DI

"Chris Field has assembl ....g stories of everyday individuals who are making a difference. These stories represent the dream, vision, and courage that live within us all if we dare to disrupt and take action."

—**Ricky Dickson,** president, Blue Bell Creameries

"We need business leaders who will solve the really big problems facing the world today—hunger, poverty, gender inequality, energy sustainability, and climate change. Chris' book is exactly the kind of disruption impetus they will need to get there. As Chris calls us to do in this book, I hope my students will disrupt the status quo and question the assumed as they pursue a new truth. I can't wait for my students to get their hands on this book."

—**Shannon Deer,** PhD, CPA, director of MBA program and senior lecturer, Texas A&M University

"As a Ghanaian, I am so thankful for the work Chris and Mercy Project are doing here in Ghana. In this book, Chris shines a light on the power of audacity, courage, selflessness, and creativity to disrupt the status quo in pursuit of social justice. This vivid journey into the lives of incredible individuals is a necessary read for anyone who wants to disrupt for good."

—**Joha Braimah,** Ghana country director, Free the Slaves

"After reading *Disrupting for Good*, I have been highly motivated to use the examples and practical steps outlined in this book to make changes in my life. Throughout my professional football career these principles have been evident, and Chris has done a great job of summarizing them in a concise and easy-to-read format."

—**Bruce Matthews,** Houston Oilers/Tennessee Titans 1983–2001, Pro Football Hall of Fame 2007

DISRUPTING
FOR GOOD

DISRUPTING
FOR GOOD

USING PASSION
AND PERSISTENCE
TO CREATE
LASTING CHANGE

CHRIS FIELD

LEAFWOOD
P U B L I S H E R S
an imprint of Abilene Christian University Press

DISRUPTING FOR GOOD
Using Passion and Persistence to Create Lasting Change

LEAFWOOD
P U B L I S H E R S
an imprint of Abilene Christian University Press

Copyright © 2018 by Chris Field

ISBN 978-1-68426-001-0

Printed in the United States of America

Scripture quotations are from The Holy Bible, New International Version®, NIV®. Copyright © 1973, 1978, 1984, 2011 by Biblica, Inc.® Used by permission. All rights reserved worldwide.

Cataloging-in-Publication Data is on file at the Library of Congress, Washington DC.

Cover design by Bruce Gore | Gore Studio, Inc.
Interior text design by Sandy Armstrong, Strong Design

Leafwood Publishers is an imprint of Abilene Christian University Press
ACU Box 29138
Abilene, Texas 79699

1-877-816-4455
www.leafwoodpublishers.com

18 19 20 21 22 23 / 7 6 5 4 3 2 1

To Famous, Micah, Beckett, Lincoln, and Theodore—
May you never forget that you're beautiful,
God made you, and you're going to change the world.
I love you.

And to Stacey—I adore you and always have.
Thank you for being the perfect first officer in this
life of disruption we've chosen. You're my favorite.

Acknowledgments

Any labor of love requires a village of people to both cheer you on and remind you why you're doing what you're doing. I had plenty of both of those as I wrote this book—more than I could ever possibly list out here. But a handful of people deserve special recognition for the role they played in helping me get this book into your hands.

Stacey—Thank you for continuing to believe in me and all my crazy dreams. You're a gift to the world.

Mom and Dad—Thank you for enduring all of those parent/teacher conferences and hearing the word "potential" a million times. You've always loved me well.

Jason Fikes—Thank you for believing in me and this story (the latter of which you believed in long before I had written enough for you to know it would be any good).

The Leafwood Publishing Team—Thank you for taking a messy manuscript and turning it into a story that people would want to read.

Don and Becky—Thank you for graciously offering your home and back porch as a writing sanctuary. It was exactly what I needed.

Gretchen—Thank you for letting me verbally process most of the ideas in this book two, or three, or four times. I owe you.

Joanna—Thank you for helping me find more details on so many of these powerful stories.

Chris White—Thank you for sending me the article on the new degree in innovation and disruption at the University of Southern California and saying it made you think of me. In doing so, you gave me a new name and helped me articulate something I'd always felt but never knew how to explain.

Mel Bowman—Thank you for hiring a nineteen-year-old kid into a job too big for him in the belief that his disruption could be a force used for good. It changed me forever.

Dean and Ronda—Thank you for always believing in me and the vision of Mercy Project. You have impacted my life more than you'll ever understand this side of heaven.

Johnny Myers—Thank you for your early help on the definitions and the MAP of disruption at the end. You are an important part of my story.

Clint and Hailey—Thank you for taking a big mess of a big dream and building it one piece at a time. You two are a special gift.

To the Ghanaian staff—Thank you for walking this long road of freedom and new life with us. Your love for your people and this mission is beautiful.

To the Mercy Project board of directors—Thank you for believing in and trusting this ministry and me. Your fingerprints are all over this story.

Contents

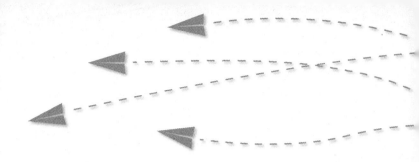

Introduction

Let's begin with the most important takeaway of this entire book: You can choose to be a disruptor, which means you have the ability to change *your* world and *the* world. Yes, you. Within you right now is everything you need to start living out the dreams you have never dared to say out loud. This is the truth—independent of your age, wealth, race, education, personality type, marital status, or current job. The purpose of this book is to convince you of this and give you the tools you need to go out and disrupt for good.

This is not a motivational book, although I hope it will motivate you. This is not an inspirational book, although I hope it will inspire you. This is not a self-help or "get rich" book, although I hope it will be helpful (and some of you will certainly use these principles to make more money). Instead, this is a book about dreaming, visioning, daring, and doing (with an emphasis on the *doing*), because our world is in desperate need of people who will talk less and do more—people who will not simply ask good questions but who will begin contributing great answers.

When I began dreaming of writing a book like this, I thought the best way to sell a bunch of copies would be to get interviews with famous people whose names we all know (e.g., Mark Cuban, Bill Gates, Mark Zuckerberg, and Michael Jordan). However, the more I thought about it, the less I liked that idea. Actually, I got to where I really hated that idea. A book that rehashed oft told and now tired stories seemed anything but disruptive. Then I realized the most disruptive (and risky) path would be to first find, and then tell, the stories of the kinds of people of whom none of us have ever heard—the disruptors who live next door. People who live on our streets, went to our colleges, shop in our grocery stores, and play in our parks. These are the kinds of stories that really spur us to action because they are stories of people just like us. Reading stories like this leaves us with no excuses. If they can do it (spoiler alert: they have), then we can too.

In the following pages, you will find plenty of stories about people rattling the cages of reality and stomping on the status quo. These are stories of ordinary people who chose to become disruptors. These are people no different from you and me. As you read, I want you to place yourself inside each one of these stories and make yourself at home. Take your shoes off, hang up your coat, and stay a while. By the end, I hope you will be comfortable enough in these stories of disruption that you'll be jumping up and down on the bed and sliding on a mattress down the stairs.

For anyone who has ever wanted more, for the person who goes to bed wondering why it all matters, for those in the world who think there has to be more to life than this, for anyone who sits in a cubicle dreaming of freedom, for everyone who sees tragedy or calamity and wishes they could fix it, for all who hunger to live a life in which their best gifts and talents are being used to the max—this book is for you. Let us journey together to discover what it means to live fully, abundantly, and with abandon. Let us journey together to discover how we can become disruptors who change the world. It is time for you to do a cannonball off the cliffs of complacency. Are you ready? Great adventures await all of us. Let's get started.

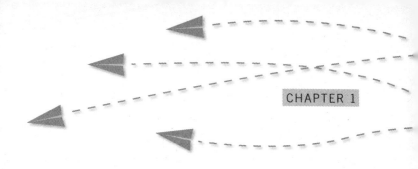

CHAPTER 1

My Friend Chris

I used to think my story of becoming a disruptor started when I ran for mayor of my hometown at age nineteen, but then I reconnected with my second-grade teacher on Facebook and was reminded of a story that took place long before my teenage mayoral campaign.

Chris was his name also, and I met him on the first day of the second grade. It was not just his first day of second grade; it was also his first day in a new school. I knew Chris was different, though I did not really know how or why.[1] What I did know was that elementary school playgrounds, hallways, and cafeterias could be an unforgiving place for a boy with a developmental delay who was more rotund than his classmates and preferred the comfort of sweat suits over the "cool" fashions the rest of us favored. I decided immediately that Chris and I would be friends, that we would stick together. For better or worse, the two Chrises were going to conquer second grade as a team.

One stroke of good luck was that Chris and I shared a teacher, an amazingly kind and generous woman named Mrs. Womack. She quickly picked up on what was happening and discreetly went out of her way to make sure Chris and I were able to be together as often as possible. Here is what Mrs. Womack remembers about our special bond: "You were wonderfully kind to Chris, always including him in activities and frequently sitting beside him. In fact, his mom told me she didn't believe how sweet the children were to him. I think he had a good year and certainly helped all of us realize that 'on the inside of our outsides' we are all the same."

I want to be clear that I do not tell this story to make myself out to be some sort of hero (in fact, I labored over including it at all because I did not want it to come across like that). There were countless other classmates I did not pursue and love as well as I did Chris. That is what makes this story stand out in my mind. When it came to my relationship with Chris, I chose to disrupt. Even as a seven-year-old, I was uncomfortable with the truth of what life in our school might be like for Chris if he did not have allies and friends to walk alongside him. So I chose to show up, I took action, and I stayed there until a new and better truth had been born. That new and better truth was our learning that Chris was more like us than he was different, and we all loved to be around him. In the strange and unspoken hierarchy of elementary school, there are accepted norms for how kids like Chris usually get treated. At worst, it is by way of bullying, taunting, and teasing. At best, it is often with indifference and exclusion.

However, we dismantled those norms and forged a previously unimagined future. A future in which Chris was fully one of us: our classmate, our peer, and our friend. That is the heartbeat of disruption.

Fast-forward a few years to my freshman year of college. Plenty of disruption had happened between second grade and the end of high school, but it would be a stretch to call most of it disruption for good. However, when I was nineteen years old, I earned my first front-page story in the local newspaper. The headline read something like "Local College Student to Run for Mayor." Here is how it all came to be: I was reading the newspaper one morning when I noticed a story about the upcoming mayoral election. The part that stood out to me the most was that the favorites to win the job were both well over sixty years old. This was in a town of about sixty thousand people, with a very young population that included many young families as well as tens of thousands of students from nearby Texas A&M University. Knowing this, I could not believe there were no younger candidates vying for the position. So I marched down to city hall to see what I needed to do to sign up. The conversation went something like this:

Me: "Hi, I would like to sign up to run for mayor."

Secretary: "Um, okay. Have you thought about starting with city council?"

Me: "I have not. Go big or go home, right?"

Secretary: "Uh, sure. Fill this out, and don't skip the part about your campaign treasurer."

21

Two minutes later, I was officially a mayoral candidate. (My friend, Tristan, was officially a mayoral campaign treasurer, a bit of news that came as a surprise to both of us.)

I did not win that election, but I did finish third out of five candidates. Most importantly, I learned the most valuable of lessons: just because it has never been done before does not mean you should *not* do it.

I was uncomfortable with the truth of two retirement-age or older candidates being the favorites to win an election in a town full of young people, so I did something about it. I showed up, I signed up, and I ran in that election to the best of my ability. The accepted norm was that someone my age was not qualified to run for mayor. In fact, people told me they thought I was playing a big joke. Of course they did! I was forging an unimagined future that they could not yet fully comprehend. The only thing I could do was stick around until that new future was made clear—and that is exactly what I did.

When the same local newspaper printed its Election Day edition a few days before the election, I was terribly anxious to see what they would say about me. I had spent more than an hour with the editorial board just a few weeks before, and I did not think it went well. I sat at one end of the table while they peppered me with questions about the city, city government, politics, and the like. I was beat when I walked out of the room, and I was sure they hated me. Imagine my surprise when I opened to their section on the mayoral campaign and read this: "Field . . . is bright, articulate, and knowledgeable of how the council

22

operates. . . . His youth and his vitality make him a person who will be a force to reckon with in years to come."[2]

That is the birth of a new truth. That is the discovery of an unimagined future. From the age of nineteen to today, I have been fortunate enough to do many cool and meaningful things: I went to college, got a couple degrees, directed a summer camp that hosted thousands of inner-city kids, worked at a Boys and Girls Club, got a scholarship to law school, quit law school, ran a bunch of marathons and ultramarathons, taught myself to be an auctioneer, wrote a children's book, organized and successfully achieved four Guinness World Records, launched the "Run for Boston 4/17" running campaign that went viral, started several businesses, founded the highest-rated marathon in the state of Texas, was asked to teach a business class at Texas A&M University, and have spoken to tens of thousands of people about pursuing their dreams and choosing to live with passion. And all of that is on the side. My full-time job over the last seven years has been helping to bring freedom to more than one hundred enslaved children in Ghana, Africa. In almost every one of these instances I was doing something my peers (and even those much older than I) were not doing. In almost every one of those instances one or a dozen people said I should not or could not achieve what I set out to accomplish, but I kept making the conscious decision to dismantle accepted norms and forge unimagined futures. I kept choosing to listen to my heart, which never failed in telling me when a current truth was simply too uncomfortable for me to continue on and ignore.

People who love you are often going to tell you hard things should not be attempted. They will say this because they are afraid to see you fail. They speak out of love and concern, but that does not make them any less wrong. It just means you should be kind when you respond to tell them you are going to go for it anyway. We will talk more about this later in the book, but I want to go ahead and acknowledge it now. It is very hard to believe we are disappointing people who care about us, but it is an inevitable part of the disruption cycle, because disruption at its core is choosing (or creating) a path that most others have no interest in pursuing or are terrified to even consider. But— and please do not miss this—*my life was changed forever when my willingness to dream and take chances outgrew my fear of failure.*

But I am getting ahead of myself here. Before we get too far into my story, or into yours, we must first understand a little bit more about the genesis of the word *disruption* and why it matters for us today. Then we will pick back up on my story and the stories of many other ordinary disruptors who are changing the world.

NOTES

[1] I was recently able to reconnect with Chris and his mother and was very happy to find out that Chris is now married, attending college, and living in Austin, Texas.

[2] Editorial Board, *The Eagle* (Bryan/College Station, TX), April 28, 2002.

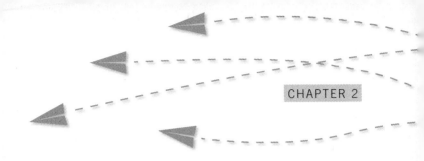

CHAPTER 2

So What Is Disruption?

The word *disruption* first become popular in the business world in the late 1990s when an esteemed Harvard professor named Clay Christensen used the word in his book.[1] The exact phrase Christensen used was "disruptive innovation," and he used it to describe what happens when an innovation creates "a new market" that disrupts the existing market into which that product has come. Since his introduction of this word, it's been used time and time again. There have been numerous articles, books, and journals written on the topic. Lots of business types even believe the word has been beaten to death. What I find fascinating is that the word has by and large remained alive and well only in the business sector and never really made its way over to the rest of the population. That is a shame because it is a word and an idea that holds an incredible amount of power and relevance for all of us, because it is disruptors who have always changed, and are still changing, the world.

First things first, we need to address the proverbial elephant in the room: disruption is not a bad thing. I know, I know, your first grade teacher, Sunday school leader, and super strict Aunt Sally all seemed to disagree when you were a rambunctious kid, but here is the definition of *disrupt* straight from the pages of Webster's dictionary:

> *Disrupt*—To cause something to be unable to continue in the normal way; to interrupt the normal progress or activity of something.

As you can see, there is nothing inherently negative about the word *disruption* unless we believe that normal progress should never be interrupted, and I doubt that very many of us believe that. Remember, at one time in history normal progress would have included realities like no electricity or running water, separate water fountains for people of different ethnicities, and horse-drawn carriages. So normal progress being interrupted, the definition of *disrupt*, is exactly what has kept our world moving forward in remarkably important ways since long before any of us were born.

Think of all the disruptors it took just for me to get this book into your hands: one to create the alphabet, two more to create paper and then ink, yet another to insist on education for all children, someone else who brought us computers and word processors, and finally, at least one more who dreamed up the Internet, which is likely where you both heard about and purchased this book. So the first point on which we need to agree is that normal progress can and should be interrupted when it is appropriate to do so.

The entire premise of this book is that disruption is necessary, appropriate, and even good much more often than we tend to believe. Disruption is needed for anyone, anywhere, who wants to interrupt the normal progress of something. In other words, disruption is what needs to happen when we do not like the trajectory of a particular thing, idea, or movement.

Dissatisfied in a relationship with a friend, coworker, or spouse? Become a disruptor.

Frustrated with where you find yourself financially? Become a disruptor.

Disgruntled with some problem or challenge you see in the world? Become a disruptor.

Unwilling to raise your children in the same way you were raised? Become a disruptor.

Yes, it is that simple. There is no lack of things that need to be disrupted, but there is a lack of willingness and understanding of how to become that disruptor. This book is going to empower and equip you to solve real problems that will help the world become a better place to live.

I have come up with two definitions for disruptors that we will revisit throughout this book. The first is that *a disruptor is someone who dismantles accepted norms and forges unimagined futures.* Read that again. What stands

)w does that sit with you? Please note, people who only dismantle accepted norms are not disruptors. Those kinds of people are destructors, and our world has more of those people than it could ever need. Disrupting is not tearing down for the sake of tearing down; it is tearing down with the intent to create and shape a better, and never before seen, way forward. In this way, being a disruptor means you will start by dismantling but always follow that up with the construction of a previously unimagined future. Disruption sometimes requires the brute strength of a sledgehammer, but it always requires the patience and careful touch of a seasoned brick mason.

The second definition we will revisit throughout the book is this: *disruptors are uncomfortable with a current truth—so they show up, take action, and persist until a new and better truth has been born.*[2] I really like this definition because it addresses two of the most important pieces of disruption: seeing and acting. Disruptors have the vision to see something that makes them uncomfortable and the courage to persist until they have helped birth a new truth. In this way, disruptors are a bit like a doula. My friend Heather is a certified doula, which means she supports women in labor. Heather's role during a delivery is to empower, encourage, and advocate for the mom. No matter how long it takes, she is there until the very end. She cheers the mother on, curses under her breath with her, and often even cries with her. This is not all that different from the journey of a disruptor. If current truths were simple or easy to change, they would have been changed already, but disruptors choose to stay all the way until the very end, no matter how long it takes. They empower, encourage, and support this new and better truth. This may include cheering on, cursing under one's breath, and even crying. But when that new truth is born, everyone rejoices because something that has never existed before is now seen and fully appreciated by the world.

My experience tells me that the way these definitions sit with you will depend largely on how and where you find it most comfortable to sit. This is precisely why I included two definitions instead of just one. Some of you will read the first definition with strong language about dismantling and forging new futures and think, *Oh, that's not me. I'm more of a go-with-the-flow type of person.* Others will read that language and think, *YES! Let's kick those doors down and make it happen.* Neither is right or wrong—just a reflection of the life experiences and likely the personality and nature of the person saying them. In the same way, some of you will read the second definition and think, *Aha! That's me. I'm a steady Eddie who always shows up and is willing to stay as long as needed.* Others will read that language and think, *NO! That sounds boring and like it might take forever. Let's go forge some new paths instead.* Again, neither one of those is right or wrong, just a mini-mirror that might help you think through where you are coming from when you approach the topic of disruption.

One point I do want to make clear is that those definitions are not as different as you might think, and they certainly do not stand in contrast to one another. They are simply two different ways of looking at the same process of bringing about change and transformation. Yes, becoming a disruptor means dismantling accepted norms and forging an unimagined future, but it also means showing up and sticking around until that new and better truth (a.k.a. unimagined future) has been born. You will find in the stories throughout this book that people who become disruptors do so not by following one of those definitions over the other but by choosing all of the above—which brings us back to my own personal story, the next part of which takes place in Ghana, Africa. It was here that my willingness to dismantle, forge, show up, and persist would be put to the ultimate test.

NOTES

[1] Clayton M. Christensen, *The Innovator's Dilemma: The Revolutionary Book That Will Change the Way You Do Business*, reprint edition (New York: Harper Business, 2011).

[2] Special thanks to my friend Johnny Myers for helping with this definition one morning over coffee at his favorite local bakery.

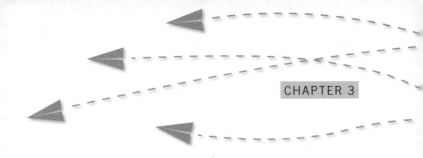

CHAPTER 3

Tomas

Ghana, Africa, is an amazing place filled with some of the most gracious, kind, and generous people I have ever met. My friend Pam Cope nailed it when she said the Ghanaians have a hospitality that would put Martha Stewart to shame. Ghanaians have literally offered me the food off of their plates, the shirts off of their backs, and the money out of their shallow pockets. There is a depth of compassion in the country that runs as deep as the rust-colored dirt roads run long. However, every good story has a villain, and the villain in Ghana is poverty—chew you up, spit you out, and leave you gasping for air on the side of the road poverty. While Ghana is better off economically than much of sub-Saharan Africa, it is still filled with many millions of people who struggle and fight just to survive. Because of this, the country's most vulnerable population, women and children, often find themselves in unthinkable situations. Ghana is also home to the world's largest man-made lake, a lake on which an estimated seven to ten thousand of these vulnerable children work every day as child slaves.

In 2009, I was on the hunt for my next adventure. What I didn't know then (but know now) is that I was searching for a current truth that would make me so uncomfortable I would feel compelled to act. I want to be clear: I was not looking for a job (had one of those), was not looking for a place to go (had just bought a house), and was not looking for a big change to my family life (we had just found out my wife was pregnant with our first baby). Rather, I was looking for something into which I could pour my gifts, passions, and talents. I was searching for an accepted norm that I believed to be unsatisfactory. I was looking for a new place to forge a currently unimagined future. And boy, did I find it—first on the pages of a book and then in dozens of rickety wooden boats on a huge lake in Ghana.

I have read hundreds of books over my lifetime. None have impacted the direction of my life like the one I read in May of 2009. It was a book called *Jantsen's Gift* by Pam Cope, and it told the story of children in Ghana, Africa, who worked all day on fishing boats. As soon as I read the book, I was agonizingly uncomfortable with the current truth it illuminated. Kids as slaves? Parents so poor and desperate they sell their children? I could not even wrap my mind around it, but I knew I could not walk away. I immediately Googled the author's name, found her phone number, and called her. I do not remember all the details of that first conversation, but I know I wanted, I needed, to convey to her that I felt compelled to do something to help. Ninety days later I stepped off an airplane and onto the ground of Ghana, Africa, for the first time—and my life would never be the same again.

It was on that trip to Ghana that I began meeting the young boys and girls who spent their long days on rickety wooden fishing boats. They were children in age and size but had hands like an old Texas rancher—swollen and calloused hands that had already held more than a lifetime of fishing nets, paddles, and hooks. Hands that were soon wrapped around my heart with no intention of letting go. I spent that first trip soaking it all in and doing my best to hold myself together. I was simultaneously captivated and being broken by what I saw. At no point was that more true than in the story of young Tomas.

Tomas was a little boy, probably around nine years old, whose village we visited near the end of the trip. The group I was with was trying to negotiate with his master for his release, which left Tomas and me sitting together for about an hour. We could not communicate, not with words anyway, but we did not need to. He was hoping for the best. I was too. He reached over and took my hand at one point and held it like only a desperate child daring to dream of a future would do. I will spare you the play-by-play (and I am honestly not even sure what happened), but the negotiations eventually broke down. Tomas was not going anywhere that day and maybe not ever. We turned to leave, and many of the children from the village followed us as we walked back down to our boat. I could not find Tomas anywhere. My eyes searched back to where we had been sitting, and I finally saw him. His head was leaning against a wooden pole, and the look in his eyes haunts me to this day. His empty eyes said, "Of course it didn't work. Why did I ever expect anything else? I'll be here, working, forever." I turned away quickly so no one would see my tears.

I returned home just a few days later and vividly remember sitting on the couch talking with my wife about the trip. My wife, Stacey, was six months pregnant with our first child, a little girl, and we had recently decided we would name her Micah. Her name comes from one of our favorite verses in the Bible, Micah 6:8, which basically says, "What does God want you to do? Act with justice, love mercy, and walk with him." I remember looking at my wife's stomach and thinking, "How could I ever ask this child to act with justice and love mercy if I'm not willing to do the same?" The answer soon became clear: We could not do that. We would not do that. My wife and I were uncomfortable with a current truth. So we showed up, took action, and stayed until a new truth was born. We named that new truth Mercy Project.

Our initial response was not that different from a lot of well-resourced people who want to help: we set out to fundraise with the intention of giving that money to an organization that was already working in Ghana. So for almost nine months we told everyone we knew about the story of the kids in Ghana. We made a short video on our home computer, we mailed letters to friends and family, I connived eight of my friends into running a 240-mile relay from Dallas to Houston, and we attempted (and succeeded in) our first Guinness World Record event—fifty consecutive hours of kickball. We kept finding ways to tell the story, and we kept raising money as we went. This was all good and well until we discovered a new truth that once again left us uncomfortable: we could not find a single group in Ghana that was attacking the issue of child slavery in a way that we thought might actually solve it forever. We could give all that hard-raised money away, but we could not be sure it would actually make a sustainable difference.

There are a number of well-regarded organizations working in Ghana, but most of their solutions do not come close to matching the complexity of the problem of child trafficking and modern-day slavery in Ghana. In fact, many of the solutions could be creating unintended consequences that could inadvertently create more child trafficking. We searched high and low for how we might overcome this and came to a sobering realization: many nonprofits make people feel good, but most are not equipped to solve problems forever. Working yourself out of a job should be near the top of every nonprofit's to-do list, but it usually is not even on the radar. Let me be clear: I believe the majority of nonprofits are started with the good intentions of making a difference, but they are rarely started with the foresight, long-term planning, and complex thinking needed to actually eradicate the problems they set out to solve. Most of the thought leaders are in the for-profit sector, because that is where thought-leading is best incentivized. When this happens, there becomes a great divide, with deep-feeling, big-hearted people on one side and deep-thinking, big-problem-solving people on the other. Could we bridge that gap in a way that would help the children of Ghana become free? We were about to find out because *every previously unimagined future begins with a single step*.

I left my job and started as Mercy Project's lone employee on September 1, 2010. Truth be told, I was terrified. I had no idea what I was doing. I was overwhelmed by the scope of the problem. I was terrified with the thought of engaging an issue that seemed too large to actually solve. So what did I do with those fears and doubts and worries? I named them. Fear did not rule me because I gave it a name and called it out. I told my wife, and my mom, and my best friends, "Man, this is crazy. I hope this works." They affirmed and encouraged and inspired me to pursue this vision. They recalled my other crazy ideas that had worked and reminded me that it would not define me if I did fail. That failing, especially when pursuing something noble and good and right, was okay—I would be the same guy after a failure that I was before it. I needed to hear that. I used it to catapult me forward as I leapt off that crowded cliff of complacency to do a cannonball into the sea of big dreams and bold ideas. Our big dream and bold idea was that we could build a new kind of nonprofit from the ground up—a nonprofit that functioned with the problem-solving ability and financial acumen of a business while also being led by hearts of compassion and mercy. We wanted to build something that would eventually work us out of a job. We were going to disrupt child trafficking in Ghana, but we would not stop there. We also wanted to disrupt the way all nonprofits and their donors created their processes to try to bring about lasting and long-term change.

Let me make a confession here: I knew that I wanted to help, but I did not know where to begin. My background was in traditional nonprofits, which meant I loved the idea of solving problems differently but had no real experience in doing that. Enter my friend Dean: a very successful businessman, married to my wife's cousin, who had heard about my newfound passion at a time when he himself was in search of a meaningful challenge. Our wives insisted we had met before, but neither of us had made enough of an impression on the other to remember. Dean is about twenty years older than me, has two business degrees, and has run multiple large companies. I have two liberal arts degrees and had never read a business book. We began to talk, and while we didn't have a name for it at the time, our conversations centered on the idea of social entrepreneurship. Dean and I were a great pair; he was a seasoned and veteran problem solver, and I was a young dreamer with limitless energy and passion. We both knew what was happening in Ghana was complex and messy and that current methods aimed at solving these problems simply were not working. It was time to roll up our sleeves and help deliver a new and better truth.

Let me briefly explain the journey Mercy Project has been on since our inception. These are some, but not all, of the ways we have shown up, taken action, and stayed until a new truth could be born. This is the unimagined future we have helped forge. This is our model of disruption.

The first thing we did in Ghana was to take the posture of being learners. This was their country and their children, not ours. We did not march into the country armed with assumptions based on our culture and values. We entered a new place, among a new people, and we listened. We watched. We asked questions. For nearly a year, this was all we did. We wanted to understand the problem inside and out, and we wanted to understand it from the mouths of the very people who were living in and around it.

Second, we committed to long-term solutions, even though we knew they would be harder, take longer, and be more expensive. We were also very honest with our donors about this reality (and pleasantly surprised by their positive response).

Third, we knew that we simply could not bring simplistic solutions to solve massive, multigenerational problems. So we did not even try, and this pushed us into thinking more creatively about the problem.

Fourth, we realized there was no "bad guy," and there did not have to be. Villains are often lazy stand-ins for more difficult problems—an easy target to generate sympathy and funds. We were told the bad guys were the fishermen who owned the children. We disagreed. The "bad guy" is poverty and lack of opportunity and education. To identify this deeper enemy is to begin attacking the real issues. Our theory was confirmed when we found that nearly 70 percent of the fishermen in our first partner village had been trafficked children themselves. It was a vicious cycle that would never be solved by vilifying those who were once victims of the cycle themselves.

We set out to create a process in Ghana that is disruptive in every way. We are literally teaching the fishermen who own the children a new and better way to fish (aquaculture). We are gifting these villages with a business and teaching them how to be businesspeople. We are inviting them to walk alongside us as we work together to solve this problem. We are allowing them to be a part of the solution rather than naming them as the problem, and we are witnessing the fishermen go on a journey from shame to pride as they see their own participation in the problem as a critical part of helping to eradicate it. But the disruption does not end there.

We also became very uncomfortable with how other groups were handling the few children they did manage to rescue. Some were placing them in long-term care facilities where they effectively became orphans with no connection to their biological families, while others were just showing back up at the parents' houses and handing the children over without any process of rehabilitation and follow-up. We did not believe either one of those was best for the kids or sustainable, so we set out to birth yet another new truth. You see, disruption is rarely a one-time event. Once you begin to see and feel truths that make you uncomfortable, you will often find your whole life gets turned upside down. Not only are you seeing things you have never before seen, but you also begin to feel equipped and empowered to be the one who makes the changes you know need to happen.

The children we help free from the labor of the fishing villages first spend three to six months in a rehabilitation shelter where, for the first time, they have their emotional, medical, and physical needs fully met. While they are there, we begin working with the families of the children to help prepare them for the return and reunification of their children. We do this because we believe an empowered and equipped parent is the best caregiver for the child she has brought into this world. We do this because not only do we want to set children free, but we want to help entire families experience freedom from financial bondage. Our work in Ghana has shown us, time and time again, that parents are willing to take care of their children but often do not feel capable or equipped to do so. Not only is investing in their capabilities and equipping usually better for both the parents and their children, but it is also much more sustainable and has a positive effect that will last for generations. Further, parents who feel capable of caring well for their children, and children who feel genuinely cared for by their parents, are significantly less likely to ever be retrafficked.

To date, Mercy Project has rescued, rehabilitated, and reintegrated more than one hundred children. Not one of them has been retrafficked, and all of them attend school or receive vocational training.

This process is the reason that other nonprofits, which are twenty times our size, are calling to ask us how we are doing what we are doing. This is the kind of disruptive thinking that led to a guy who has never taken a business class being asked to teach a business class at one of the top business schools in America. But I am not alone, and Mercy Project is not alone. Our world is filled with disruptors. People like me who are uncomfortable with a current truth and are willing to show up and stick around until a

new and better truth is born—people willing to dismantle accepted norms and forge unimagined futures. The
following chapters are filled with the stories of ordinary
people who disrupted the norm. People like you. People
like me. I want you to hear their stories because I believe
they will change you. I want you to "meet" them on the following pages because I believe they will inspire you. I want
you to see that ordinary people are changing the world
because I want you to believe that you can join them. I
want their dreams of disruption to help stir your own.

Are you ready?

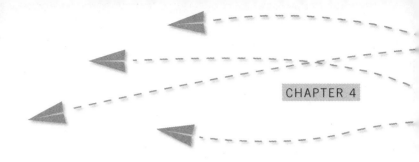

CHAPTER 4

A New Kind of Nursing Home

Close your eyes and try to remember the last time you walked into a nursing home or care center for the elderly. Try to recall the look, the feel, and the smells. For the vast majority of us, this is not a pleasant memory. Even if we were there to visit someone we really loved, maybe a friend or family member about whom we have otherwise positive memories, we typically think of nursing homes and immediately recall the many parts of that experience that make us less than comfortable. The hard tile hallways, echoing each footstep loudly. The harsh bright lights, somehow making the white paint on the walls so intense it hurt our eyes. The quiet, almost somber atmosphere. And the smells. The smells are the worst part. Walking through the doors almost immediately brings an unpleasant mix of chemicals, cleaners, and uncontrolled bodily functions. Nursing homes are really tough places to visit, to work, and surely to live. But there is another way.

Now try to imagine the piercing laughter of a child in those same nursing home hallways—the deep, true, and innocent laughter of a child without a care in the world. The laughter gets closer and the source of that joyful noise comes fully into view. It's a little boy, probably three years old, with messy blond hair in his eyes, applesauce from snack time still on his little pocketed shirt, and wearing those little boy jeans that make any kid look like a model. He is barreling down the hallway with everything he has, which reminds you of a cartoon show where the legs are spinning furiously but the character is not actually going anywhere. And hot on the little boy's tail is an elderly man in a wheelchair. As he comes into view, you hear his laughter now, too—kind, careful, and true. It is the laughter from a life that has learned not to miss a chance to smile and be glad. You watch in amusement as the little boy and the man barrel past you as though you are not even standing there. Off they go, laughter still echoing down the hallways, even when they are no longer in sight.

I know this story might seem far-fetched or unrealistic, but it is not. It is a real scenario from a real place. It is called Seattle Providence Mount St. Vincent nursing home and is located in Seattle, Washington. In many ways, it is a nursing home filled with the types of residents you likely pictured earlier, people like your grandmother or my great-grandfather. The average resident is over ninety years old, and many of them need significant help each day, as they are unable to move around without assistance from the nursing home staff.[1] Yet for more than twenty-five years now, up to 125 children a day, ages zero to five, have shared the nursing home each weekday with its elderly residents. These kids are part of the Intergenerational Learning Center (ILC), the purpose of which is "to allow kids to learn about acceptance while also being nurtured."[2] The ILC goes on to explain that "the program was designed to counterbalance the loneliness and boredom that so often characterize life in a nursing facility."[3] Harriet Thompson was a ninety-three-year-old resident at the home when she said, "I'm a great-great-grandmother, but [my family is] in another town. I can't hold my own little girl because she's far away. And so this is what makes me happy. You get to know [the kids that visit], and watch them, and act silly with them. And it's good to feel like you're three years old again."[4]

Amazingly, this unlikely marriage is not simply providing a joyful atmosphere for kids and elderly adults; it has actual benefits that go far beyond having a good time. From decreased loneliness to delayed mental decline,[5] there are a host of ways engaging with young children on a regular basis benefits the aging population. The same can be said for the children in the program as well. Marie Hoover, ILC director, says, "I've had parents call me years after their children have graduated from our program to let me know about some incident when their child was the first to warmly greet someone who happened to be in a wheelchair."[6] Elderly adults who are less lonely and more mentally robust, and young children who learn to be comfortable around the older population and carry a lifetime of lessons in empathy with them upon leaving the center—this is the ultimate win-win.

"All of us have common needs to share life together," administrator Charlene Boyd says. "And so these children bring life and vibrancy and normalcy. It's a gift. It's a gift in exposing young families to positive aspects of aging, and it's a gift of also having children seeing frailty, normalcy and that's part of the full circle of life."[7] She goes on to say, "We wanted a living, vibrant community; to make sure that this was a place where people came to live, not die."[8] *A living, vibrant community where people came to live rather than die.* That is a statement of disruption. What a powerful image of what we all hope to experience in the end years of both our lives and the lives of people who we care about the most. I cannot imagine anyone arguing against seeing this happen, but simply desiring to see it happen is not enough. Someone had to have the guts to actually come up with the idea and then fight to see it implemented! The resulting reality is what happens when a nursing home and a daycare decide they are better together than they are apart. It is the result of an accepted norm ("This is just the way nursing homes are") becoming dismantled and an unimagined future (the merger of a nursing home and a daycare) being forged. It is what happens when someone becomes uncomfortable with the truth of nursing homes being sterile and lifeless places where people go and wait to die. It is what happens when someone shows up, takes action, and stays until a new and better truth has been born. In this case, the new and better truth is a place where those at both the very beginning and the very end of their lives can share a beautiful time together—learning, exploring, tending to one another, and practicing the kind of compassion that will cultivate lives of kindness for many years to come.

What I love most about this story is that someone took an institution that makes the vast majority of us uncomfortable and uneasy and disrupted it in a way that has now benefited thousands of people. They did not paint the walls bright colors, change the flooring to something warmer, bring in a piano man, or add a nature garden. Those are all fine things, and maybe they should be done more often, but they are not the types of actions that change the very core and culture of an institution from the inside out. Those things might be creative, but they are not disruptive.

What drives me crazy about this story is that it still appears to be an isolated moment of brilliance rather than an example for others to follow. Tens of thousands of day care centers and elderly living facilities have been built in the twenty-five years since the Seattle Providence Mount St. Vincent nursing home and Intergenerational Learning Center joined forces, so why haven't more of them considered being innovative and disruptive in their approach, especially with such positive results from this case study? The answer is unfortunate but true: it is easier to do what has always been done—even if it is not the best way. It takes guts, moxie, and a willingness to put your neck out there to create new and beautiful things, but I am convinced that those things are worth the risk.

In hindsight, most anyone would likely look at this story and see what a fantastic idea it is, but validating good ideas in hindsight is not the goal. Disruptors learn how to envision and work toward good ideas before others can see them. They see those good ideas in front of them rather than behind them. This is how the world gets changed. The spectators in the stands, the armchair quarterbacks, and the Uncle Ricos of the world are not deciding the outcome of the game, but it is those actually willing to walk to the starting line that do the deciding. Those people with the courage and compassion to disrupt make lasting change. It is disruption that breaks the silence of the nursing home with the laughter of children and adults playing tag through the once hollow hallways.

NOTES

[1] Unrelated note: God bless nursing home staff. What a thankless, difficult, and often low-paying job. Many of these people are angels for loving the elderly so well.

[2] Kimberly Yam, "This Preschool inside a Nursing Home Proves True Friendship Knows No Age," *Huffington Post*, June 25, 2015. http://www.huffingtonpost.com/2015/06/24/intergenerational-learning-center-_n_7639362.html.

[3] Tiffany R. Jansen, "The Preschool inside a Nursing Home," *The Atlantic*, January 20, 2016, https://www.theatlantic.com/education/archive/2016/01/the-preschool-inside-a-nursing-home/424827.

[4] "What Happens When a Nursing Home and a Day Care Center Share a Roof?" *PBS NewsHour*, May 10, 2016, http://www.pbs.org/newshour/bb/what-happens-when-a-nursing-home-and-a-day-care-center-share-a-roof.

[5] "What Happens When a Nursing Home."

[6] Yam, "This Preschool inside a Nursing Home Proves True Friendship."

[7] "What Happens When a Nursing Home."

[8] Jansen, "The Preschool inside a Nursing Home."

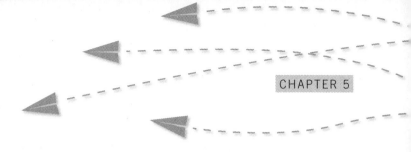

CHAPTER 5

Mama Hill

There are certain parts of Los Angeles, California, where outsiders would not want to find themselves late at night. In fact, there are some parts where it might be dangerous even in the middle of the day. These are places which have been overrun by rival and fighting gangs and riddled with crime, graffiti, bullet holes, and dashed dreams. These kinds of places are often ripe breeding grounds for an enormous amount of tragedy and despair. One such place is in the Watts neighborhood deep in Los Angeles. With 50 percent of the families living below the poverty line and only one out of every two children in the community who will graduate from high school,[1] it is the type of place most people are trying to run away from rather than run toward. But not Millicent "Mama" Hill. Mama Hill keeps running right into the chaos.

You will find Mama Hill over at 755 East 92nd Street. It is a small little place set back among the trees and barely visible from the street. When I say it is a small little place, I really mean that. It is no bigger than a small apartment, at just two bedrooms, one bathroom, and 836 total square feet.[2] But Mama Hill is not worried about the size of her place; she is worried about the children in her neighborhood—children who are too often being lost to gang violence and many others who are silent casualties of living in a neighborhood where it is unsafe to go outside and even less safe to be seen as someone showing effort in school. Dreams do not go to die on these difficult streets because they are usually not even given the chance to be born, but Mama Hill is on a mission to change that—to change all of that.

In 2001, after forty years of teaching in the Los Angeles Unified School District (the last eighteen of those years at Crenshaw High School), Mama Hill started her own nonprofit called Mama Hill's Help. Her nonprofit is an "after-school program that helps inner-city kids rise above challenges like homelessness and gang violence."[3] One of her motivations for starting the program was to help a greater number of children than the number of children she estimates she lost to violent death over her forty-year teaching career. Astonishingly, and heartbreakingly, she estimates the number of students she lost over that time to be at least two thousand.[4] As a point of reference, that would be fifty students per year or one per week over her multidecade career as an educator and friend to young people. Mama Hill became so uncomfortable with this harsh reality that she felt compelled to help a new truth be born, right there in her small little stucco house on 92nd

Street—836 square feet of tough love, new beginnings, and freshly birthed dreams.

The children who come here range in age from eight to fifteen, and there are different numbers of them in attendance every day, but they all squeeze into Mama Hill's little house among the trees and get busy learning. "The children love it here because they feel successful," says Mama Hill. "There is no such thing as a slow child," she adds. "Every child has a gift to give to the world, and it must be written on the heart with knowledge. Once a child obtains knowledge he is happy to share his gift."[5] And Mama Hill is at her best when she is writing on her students' hearts with knowledge. She has loved learning and teaching all the way back to her days as a little girl and through high school, where she graduated as the first black baccalaureate speaker of her Pasadena, California, high school in 1958. Not long after, in 1959, she joined the civil rights movement, where she endured being pelted by rocks in order to fight for equal rights for people of all races and colors.[6] Today she continues to fight for new and better truths as she comes alongside these beleaguered and long-suffering young people and invites them to walk with her into previously unimagined futures.

Understanding the deep and generationally complex layers that affect a student's success both in life and in the classroom gives Mama Hill insight into helping the whole child, which often means helping the adults who stand behind them. She frequently finds herself helping parents with their parenting and getting their own lives on track.[7] "Parents do a lot of damage because they don't know it's a trickle-down thing," Hill says. "This is how they were taught, so they're doing the same thing. Our greatest enemy is poverty and ignorance."[8] While Mama Hill may not be able to completely change the poverty component, she has dedicated her life to helping eliminate the ignorance part.

For more than fifty-six total years now, forty in the classroom and another sixteen in her own little house on 92nd Street, Hill has been putting up one heck of a fight against those unseen but ever-felt enemies of poverty and ignorance. "I provide a refuge so children can shine,"[9] Hill says, always seeming to downplay the value of her role as advisor, friend, and mentor; but those who know her best say it is a lot more than that. "She comes at everything from love and that's what she teaches these kids to do," says one of her volunteers.[10] Hill is so well-loved in her own little community that when she recently almost lost her home to foreclosure, friends, neighbors, and politicians rallied around her to help find a solution for her to be able to stay in her house. It seems the little light on the hill just cannot seem to be put out. Thank goodness.

Mama Hill's story is especially dear to me as someone who has worked extensively with inner-city youth in my life, and her steadfast devotion and unwavering commitment is absolutely mind-blowing. She has spent fifty-six of her seventy-seven years on this earth doing thankless, underappreciated, and often unpaid work for some of the most vulnerable citizens in our country. She does it with no flashy fundraisers, no fancy building (even the metal sign in her front yard with the charity name on it is so plain you almost miss it), and very little fanfare; yet she is daily exercising an incredible willingness to dismantle accepted norms (such as "Gangs are a part of life here" and "Kids from this neighborhood just do not graduate high school") and forge unimagined futures—futures in which young boys and girls can become people who accomplish things they never imagined possible. We would be hard-pressed to find better examples of someone being willing to show up, take action, and stay until a new and better truth has been born. But because of Mama Hill, that is exactly what has happened now for well over three thousand children from her Los Angeles neighborhood. These children have found a friend, confidant, and cheerleader in Mama Hill—someone they can count on and who believes in them, even when they no longer believe in themselves. Mama Hill has changed the trajectory of the lives of thousands of young people in Los Angeles, children who have become adults and now have their own children—a reminder that the steady but unflashy ripple of disruption can last for generations, even beyond what we can see or understand ourselves.

NOTES

[1] Alexandra Zaslow, "Millicent 'Mama' Hill Has 3,000 Children, and She Loves Every Single One of Them (Video)," *Huffington Post*, November 15, 2013, http://www.huffingtonpost.com/2013/11/15 /mama-hill-retired-teacher_n_4268976.html.

[2] "755 E 92nd St, Los Angeles, CA 90002," Zillow Real Estate, accessed July 20, 2017, https://www.zillow.com:443/homedetails/755 -E-92nd-St-Los-Angeles-CA-90002/20953251_zpid/.

[3] Zaslow, "Millicent 'Mama' Hill."

[4] "Local Hero: Millicent 'Mama' Hill," KCET, accessed July 20, 2017, https://www.kcet.org/local-heroes/local-hero-millicent-mama-hill-0.

[5] Valerie Shaw, "Retired Teacher Inspires At-Risk Youth," Los Angeles Community Policing, accessed July 20, 2017, http://www.lacp.org/ValShaw/TeacherInspiresYouth.html.

[6] Zaslow, "Millicent 'Mama' Hill."

[7] "Senior Saves Kids from Gang Life," NewsOne, February 23, 2012, https://newsone.com/1851545/millicent-mama-hill-saves-kids/.

[8] "Senior Saves Kids."

[9] "Senior Saves Kids."

[10] Zaslow, "Millicent 'Mama' Hill."

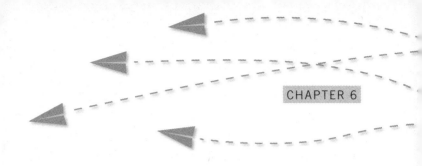

CHAPTER 6

Recycling with Micah

She was all of five years old when she came home from pre-K one day and immediately demanded to know from her parents, "Why don't we recycle?" The stammers and half-answers given were not sufficient for her, and she continued on in spite of them. "Today at school we learned all about recycling. How it helps the earth. How much trash it keeps out of landfills. How many trees it can save. And even how easy it is to do. So . . . why don't we recycle?" Her parents, now with a moment to carefully plan the strategic wording of their next answer, were ready: "We love recycling, sweetie. But we live out of town, so there is no service to pick up our recycling. But that's really cool you learned all about that today. Such an important topic."

The girl, completely unimpressed with what her parents believed to be the final answer needed, was not ready for the conversation to be over. "Why is there no service to pick up our recycling?" she pressed them. Her father, once a fiery and inquisitive little boy himself, saw the perfect opportunity to impart to her some key lessons from entrepreneurship 101. "Well, sweetie," he said confidently (poor guy had no idea), "there is no recycling service in our neighborhood because no one has started that business. Someone would have to start that business, and charge a fee, and pick it up every week to take it to the recycling center." He smiled down at her, most pleased with her silence. At last, this had satisfied her young curiosity. However, she apparently was not finished, only thinking—a most dangerous thing for young minds who are unencumbered by the weighty expectations and fears of adults. "Well then," she declared, "I'm going to start a recycling business." Just like that, Recycling with Micah was born.

The first order of business for the newly minted business owner was customer acquisition. This began by choosing the perfect brightly colored printer paper at the local office supply store. Then flyers were made, and it was time to pass them out. The neighborhood was not large, but five-year-olds have short legs. And the houses were all on acreage, with long and winding driveways. Never one to back down from a challenge, she hired her older brother (age nine) to help her at the rate of $1 per day. Each one thought they were getting the better end of the bargain—just as it should be. They hit all seventy-five houses in the first day and were exhausted but satisfied with their work. They estimated the number of takers over a snack of bananas and graham crackers.

Slowly, the emails from people ready to sign up came rolling in. After a few days, Recycling with Micah had its first fifteen customers. Micah was ecstatic. Micah's father wondered how they were going to fit it all in the minivan every week. Micah's mother told Micah's father he needed to trade his car in for a pickup truck.

Every Thursday morning, rain or shine, Micah travels around to those fifteen customers' houses and picks up their recycling. She is not always excited about going, and there are some weeks she hires her brothers to help her (the first pickup after holidays is a real doozy). She provides each of her customers with blue recycling bags each few months, and they fill them up one at a time with coke cans, plastic tubs, foil, paper, and beer bottles. For better or worse, Micah has become very observant about who "likes a lot of beer" or "had their friends over for a pizza party." Week after week she and her dad fill up the back of her mom's minivan with somewhere between fifteen and thirty bags of recycling. Then they haul it all over to the city's recycling center where their friend, Mr. Burger, stops his bulldozer to greet them and help them unload. To date (eighteen months at the writing of this book), Micah has recycled more than ten thousand pounds of would-be garbage (that's the equivalent of three hundred thousand aluminum cans) and saved up enough money to pay for her first semester of college (which she will start in eleven years). And her father, finally, just got that pickup truck her mother asked him about ten thousand pounds of recycling ago.

Micah's story reminds us that there is no age limit or educational qualification for becoming a disruptor. You don't even need to be old enough for kindergarten. You only need to be willing to dismantle an accepted norm ("Our neighborhood doesn't have a recycling service") and forge an unimagined future. Even five-year-olds can become uncomfortable with a current truth, and they'll probably solve those truths if we move out of their way and stop projecting our own fears of failure and excuse-making on top of them. Worst case, they will fail and learn something from it that will help them the next time around.

For many of us, our age, bank account balance, education level, age of our children, or career pecking order keeps us from disrupting some truth we find uncomfortable. Micah's story reminds us that this is unnecessary. At best, it is misplaced concern. At worst, it is a convenient excuse that keeps us from taking risks and putting ourselves out there.

Micah is now a timeworn and wise seven-year-old who is really showing her age. She has this advice for anyone who is scared to fail: "Just do your best. Try your hardest. And if you fail, you can just try something else." Wise words for each of us at any age.

Full disclosure: Micah is my daughter, and I am the dad in the story who finally got the truck.

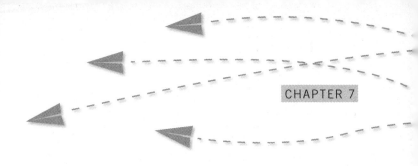

CHAPTER 7

Clara Loses It

I t is no secret that Americans today face some very significant challenges when it comes to leading healthy lives. I will save all the gory statistics, but the combination of more sedentary lifestyles coupled with easy access to thousands upon thousands of delicious foods (most of them not good for us) has created nothing short of a health epidemic in our country. It does not work in our favor that at any time, night or day, we are just a few clicks away from being able to have most any food we can imagine delivered hot and fresh right to our front door. It is a convenience that is killing us. Every weight has a counterweight, so it should come as no surprise that the health and fitness industry in America is enormous—like almost $26 billion a year enormous.[1] As a reference point, that is more than $80/year for every man, woman, and child in America. But even the rapid growth of the health and fitness industry has not been enough to slow the obesity rate and health challenges facing our country, and that is exactly what makes stories like Clara Williams's so incredibly powerful.

Clara says she started struggling with her weight all the way back in second grade. In many ways, this part of her story is not unique. There are a great number of people who can remember all the way back into elementary school as the time when they began straining to maintain healthy bodies. But Clara's difficulties with her weight did not end with high school graduation; they were just beginning. Standing five feet and ten inches tall, Clara weighed 220 pounds by the time she got married at age twenty-one. She was up to 300 pounds when she had her daughter five years later. And then, in 2010, she got on the scale at her doctor's office and saw her weight of 426 pounds.[2] It was the biggest number she had ever seen while standing on a scale, but even that number on the scale right in front of her was not enough to motivate Clara to a much-needed drastic life change. It was not until the birth of Clara's first grandson, Isaac, that she forced herself to consider that her unhealthy lifestyle was stealing years away from her life. "I knew that I would not be around for him, or the rest of my family, if I didn't get my weight under control. It was hard to even get up off the couch by myself, let alone with a baby in my arms. I was sick of being sick and tired. So I decided to fight to live life to its fullest."[3] Clara's being sick of being sick and tired is where her unique story veers off from the stories of so many others. This is where Clara's story becomes amazing and inspiring enough to be featured in a book like this. Clara decided to disrupt the vicious cycle of obesity and unhealthiness that had plagued her for decades. She became so uncomfortable with the truth that her weight was keeping her from living her life to the fullest that she showed up and was finally ready to take action.

First, she joined a nonprofit weight-loss support group at her local recreation center. She credits the encouragement and support of that group, along with the accountability of weekly weigh-ins and contests, with saving her life.[4] However, just joining a support group was not going to be enough. This is why our disruption definition does not end with showing up. Clara also had to begin taking action and taking ownership of the foods she was putting into her body. Clara began this part of her journey by making better food choices, which started by replacing junk food with natural foods that come from the earth. Then she began taking evening walks with a friend and doing exercise tapes with coworkers during her lunch break. Clara completely and totally changed her life and lifestyle in every way. She exchanged poor habits for healthy ones and unhealthy lifestyle choices for ones that would help her get her life back, but it was not always easy and did not come quickly. "I knew that as long as I was making the choice to eat healthy foods that God made and using the body he gave me to move each day, I would make it to my goal eventually. Sometimes my progress seemed slow, but I always reminded myself that I was better than where I started," she says.[5] Day after day after day, Clara showed up and took action—one moment at a time, one meal at a time, and one mile at a time. In this way, her journey was a long one—a very, very long one.

There were no shortcuts, no tricks, no secret pills or potions. She was working every day to undo the damage and poor health choices she had been making for forty years. The new truth she was working to bear required a long and difficult labor, but she remained focused on the goal at hand and celebrated the small victories as they came. When all was said and done, Clara had lost an astonishing 243 pounds (nearly 60 percent of her original body weight). Her new and better truth was born, and it was the healthier and happier version of herself she had set out to find at the start of her journey.

If you ask Clara what is different about life after her weight loss, she is able to give an entire list of answers. From the practical (fitting into seats at the movie theater and not being turned away to ride a rollercoaster) to the more long-term (no more medicine for high blood pressure or diabetes).[6] Best of all, she finally realizes what it feels like to feel good. A feeling she did not even know she was missing out on for so many years of her life. A feeling best encapsulated in her ability to play with her grandson for hours upon end at the neighborhood park. Clara set out to become healthier so that she could live longer for her family, but what she discovered along the way was that she was also paving the way to live more fully and abundantly for those extra years. Clara's advice for anyone looking to make a significant change? "Never put off until tomorrow what you can do today . . . small changes will bring you great rewards. Make a choice each day to eat healthy foods that are good for your body, and move each day—even if it's ten minutes at a time. Everything worthwhile in life is hard."[7] *Everything worthwhile in life is hard*—underline that, remember it, and come back to it often. There is an entire book that could be written from those six words!

Clara's story is powerful because it personifies the disruption process in all of its stages. She became uncomfortable with the truth of how her weight and health were hurting her, so she showed up, took action, and stayed until a new truth was born. The $26 billion health and fitness industry offers thousands of ways to lose weight—and she chose the one that took the longest but was the most sustainable. She disrupted the version of herself that was stealing years from her own life. It did not come quickly, but she persisted because Clara knew the end results would be worth it.

For many of us, Clara's story should be a helpful reminder that we should more carefully steward how we treat our bodies. This rings true, whether we need to lose two hundred-plus pounds or simply fuel our bodies with more foods that come from the earth. Even more than the food component, Clara's story gently reminds us that disruption that matters, that really makes a difference, will likely come at a cost—a daily, sometimes hourly, cost that we should not take for granted or dismiss too easily. As has been said before, if you want to get where you have always gone, then do what you have always done. But if you want to get to new places, you will have to do new things—not once, not twice, but every day for a long time. In this way, disruption is a journey. It is a long road filled with exciting opportunities to live your fullest life—the kind of life that lets you chase your grandkids around the park.

NOTES

[1] "Global Fitness Industry Records Another Year of Growth," IHRSA, accessed August 28, 2017, http://www.ihrsa.org/news/2016/5/25/global-fitness-industry-records-another-year-of-growth.html.

[2] "Clara's 243-Pound Weight Loss: 'Never Put Off until Tomorrow What You Can Do Today,'" Yahoo Health, accessed July 20, 2017, https://healthmagazine-1677-yahoopartner.tumblr.com/post/132092389787/claras-243-pound-weight-loss-never-put-off.

[3] "Clara's 243-Pound Weight Loss."

[4] "Clara's 243-Pound Weight Loss."

[5] "Clara's 243-Pound Weight Loss."

[6] "Clara's 243-Pound Weight Loss."

[7] "Clara's 243-Pound Weight Loss."

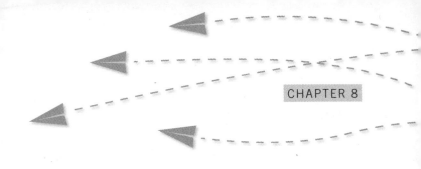

CHAPTER 8

Jen and Ted's Excellent Adventure

We've all had that moment. You know the one I am talking about. When we come home from an awful day at work or school and proclaim with a heavy sigh to our wife, boyfriend, cat, dog, or just the universe: "We should just sell everything we own and travel the world. That would be so much better than what we are doing right now!" Typically this dramatic announcement has all the fanfare of receiving our monthly cable bill in the mail and is quickly dismissed in favor of a TV dinner, story time with our kids, or our favorite Netflix series. I say *typically* because there are people like Jen and Ted Avery of Thrifty Nomads who say, "We should just sell everything we own and travel the world," and then follow that proclamation up by actually, well, selling everything they own and traveling the world. This is their story of disruption.

Jen and Ted are just like you and me. Or at least they were, until January 3, 2013, when they squeezed their remaining possessions into a couple of backpacks and set off on an adventure around the world. But let me back up a little bit before I get too far ahead of myself.

Jen and Ted were high school sweethearts from Canada who started dating in 2005. That went so well that they went ahead and got married in 2010.[1] They settled down in Toronto, where they both had "multiple jobs, commitments, and years' worth of junk stored in [their] home."[2] But it was actually a trip they took together to the United States to visit Las Vegas and the Grand Canyon that stirred a sense of adventure and freedom in them that continues to brew to this very day. "Coming from Canada, the desert landscapes were starkly different from anything we had ever seen before. The red dirt, neon sunsets, and quirky Las Vegas—it was all so new. When we got home, we couldn't stop replaying the incredible scenery in our minds. It was that trip which made us itch to keep seeing more," Ted says.[3] It did not happen immediately, but eventually the couple "decided to take the plunge, sell all of [their] possessions, quit [their] jobs, and travel long-term."[4]

But first, they had to take care of the years' worth of junk stored in their home (their words, not mine!). Now there are several options for how one might choose to go about downsizing for a trip like this. One end of the spectrum would be to purge almost nothing, store almost everything, and always have it waiting for you when you return home. This would clearly be the safest and most conservative option. On the other end of the spectrum would be what Jen and Ted did. Sell everything, literally everything, except what fits into two 28L backpacks (small enough for an airplane carry-on). Rather than feeling overwhelmed by this lack of physical possessions, Ted says, "It was the most empowering thing we had ever done, and we had never felt more free."[5] Now that they had literally sold virtually everything they owned, it was time for Jen and Ted to travel the world.

To date, they have spent time in a number of countries across South America and Europe, been to Japan, and even lived in Australia for a year. They have hiked Machu Picchu in Peru, ridden a camel through the Sahara Desert, sat with turtles in the Galapagos Islands, and ridden trains through the Japanese Alps (confession: I didn't even know Japan had alps).[6] In Ted's words, it has all been very worth it: "These are all experiences that have been more meaningful than any academic or career accomplishment in my life. There is simply no better experience for me than seeing the world."[7]

So you might be reading all of this and find yourself thinking, *That's great. These people have been on some cool vacations. But how exactly is this disruptive?* I'm glad you asked. Ted sums it up well with this quote: "Everyone says to follow your dreams and live life to the fullest, but I felt like I was one of the few who discovered what it meant to really do it. . . . I've discovered the difference between settling for a lifestyle which I have no passion for versus pursuing something that I really love."[8]

Jen and Ted, whether they would have articulated it in this exact way or not, were uncomfortable with the truth that this big, amazing, incredible world was only meant to be seen in one-week vacations once each year for the duration of their working life. They were uncomfortable with the truth that working, buying stuff, and filling up a house or apartment with said stuff was the objective of their lives. So they showed up, took action, and created a new and better truth.

Now not everyone will draw the same conclusions Jen and Ted did. Some people have no interest in traveling. Some people feel very content in working and living their lives without ever leaving their own little town. And while I would argue that traveling and engaging people from other cultures is one of the most meaningful ways we can learn about ourselves and the world, that is not the topic of this book. Rather, Jen and Ted's story reminds us that having intentionality and purpose in the ways we spend our time matters. If working and living your life without leaving your own town is what you choose to do, great. *As long as it's a purposed and intentional decision rather than a default.* Just make sure it is a conscious choice you make rather than something that you allow to happen *to* you. Ted says it like this, "I know I can make my life into anything I want it to be, so it's a blessing to constantly be conscious of how I am spending my time."[9]

What Jen and Ted did that I find so refreshing (and disruptive) is go against the status quo in having the courage and mettle to pursue their dreams. There were no doubt dozens of objections they could have cited as legitimate reasons for not doing what they ultimately made the decision to do: money (or lack thereof), risk, career suicide, safety, family, friends, and so on, and so forth. Ted actually says this is one of the pieces of feedback they get most frequently: "One of the things I hear most commonly is 'I could never do what you're doing, because I have a career.' Or school. A house. A family. There will always be a million reasons holding you back from changing your life. *No matter where you are in life, it's never impossible to make a change as long as you have the courage to try*" (emphasis mine).[10] In other words, there will always be a million reasons holding you back from disrupting some truth that makes you uncomfortable. You just have to have the courage to try.

Let me be clear: Jen and Ted are not the first people to sell everything they own to travel the world. But I love their story because it is too simple to have really any objections. They were not born into wealth, and they did not sell a business and use that money to travel. In fact, they actually travel very inexpensively (their personal blog and travel website is titled "Thrifty Nomads" for a reason). Jen and Ted are just like you and me. Or at least they were. What separates them from many of us is simply their courage to pursue their dreams and go after things that feel most meaningful to them. What makes them different from many of us is their intentionality in the manner in which they chose to spend their time. No excuses, no justification, no apologies to those they leave behind. This is the heart of disruption—a truth that makes us so uncomfortable we are willing to show up, take action, and stick around until a new and better truth is born. For Jen and Ted, that new truth is a life of travel where they are exposed to new cultures and make new friends. For us, it might look totally different. But it will always require courage. It will always require our willingness to live our lives as active participants rather than passive observers. Ted puts it this way: "We went from a life of reasons to say no to opportunities to say yes."

Disruption is learning to say yes. Yes to things that matter the most to us. Yes to things that make us feel most alive. Yes to lives of purpose and intention and significance. Jen and Ted's story offers us a beautiful example of that kind of disruption.

NOTES

[1] Lauren Pelley. "Feel Like Taking a Risk? It Could Be Contagious," *The Star*, May 31, 2016, https://www.thestar.com/life/2016/05/31/feel-like-risk-taking-it-could-be-contagious.html.

[2] Ted Avery, "How Travelling the World Changed My Life," *Ted Avery* (blog), July 26, 2014, https://medium.com/@tedavery/how-travelling-the-world-changed-my-life-1ea5ece4cf61.

[3] Mic Florendo, "Meet Jen and Ted of Thrifty Nomads [Interview]," *Vroom Vroom Vroom Car Rental Blog*, May 11, 2016, https://blog.vroomvroomvroom.com/2016/05/meet-canadian-bloggers-jen-and-ted-of-thrifty-nomads-interview.html.

[4] Florendo, "Meet Jen and Ted."

[5] Avery, "How Travelling the World."

[6] Avery.

[7] Avery.

[8] Avery.

[9] Avery.

[10] Avery.

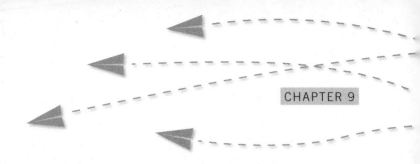

CHAPTER 9

Signs

Imagine, for a moment, that you are at your job. If you do not currently work, try to recall a job you have had somewhere along the way. Remember where you sit or stand, what your desk or workspace looks and feels like, and what kinds of things you spend your time doing. Now recall for me how you most frequently interact with your customers and coworkers. What kinds of conversations do you have? What types of information and stories do you need to convey? What sorts of problems or challenges are you helping them solve? Now I want you to imagine doing everything you just imagined without the ability to either speak or hear. Pause and think about that for a second before reading on. What you just imagined is the difficult but real life of the working deaf. The scenario you have just considered is not hypothetical for the deaf; it is their daily reality. It is a challenging world in which jobs are scarce, even for those qualified in every way other than

71

being able to speak and hear, as so many of us so often take for granted.

The United States has an estimated nine million people who would be considered deaf or hard of hearing. Of those, an estimated 75 percent are unemployed, with another 19 percent underemployed.[1] That leaves a measly 6 percent of deaf Americans who are appropriately employed in a job that fits their skills and qualifications. Put another way, just six out of every one hundred deaf or hard of hearing Americans are working in a job that best suits their qualifications and abilities. This is a shockingly low number—and these numbers are the same or even worse in other countries across the world, including our neighbors to the north in Canada. But there is one man in Toronto, Canada, who became so uncomfortable with the truth of how difficult it is for the deaf to find work that he did something about it. Something incredible. This is his story of disruption.

Anjan Manikumar was managing a Boston's Pizza in a Toronto neighborhood when he "noticed deaf customers were frequently let down and staff struggled to communicate with them."[2] Since none of the staff at his restaurant knew sign language, the deaf customers who came in had to order their food and drinks by way of pointing and nodding.[3] This bothered Anjan so much that he began to use his time outside of work to learn the basics of American Sign Language. One day, he was able to put his hard work to the test when a deaf customer came in to the restaurant to eat. Their exchange went even better than Anjan could have imagined. "The customer—who was used to mostly pointing out pictures or words to place his orders—was so overjoyed to find Anjan taking his order and telling him to enjoy his food using signs that he came back with friends the next day."[4] In that moment, a new idea was birthed in Anjan. If it was this difficult for the deaf community to be customers, how much more difficult must it be for them to be the employees? The answer, as seen in the various numbers and statistics you read previously, is extraordinarily difficult. This was a reality that bothered Anjan even more than deaf customers having to place their orders by way of pointing at pictures on the menu. It was a truth that made him so uncomfortable that he was unwilling to sit idly by and not try to do something about it.

Over the next few years, Manikumar began laying the groundwork for a new kind of restaurant. Not just a place where the deaf could come and order their food with sign language (which would be great in and of itself!), but a place where the deaf could actually come and find work, taking orders (from the deaf and the hearing) in their native sign language. The restaurant was called Signs.

It opened in the summer of 2014 in a busy part of Toronto, and it was Canada's first restaurant to employ a staff that was majority deaf. When Manikumar placed ads announcing the open staff positions at his disruptive new restaurant, *hundreds* from the deaf community applied. Those numbers were validation not only that there was a critical need for jobs for the deaf, but also that many of them were enthusiastic about gaining employment in jobs they could actually have a chance to succeed in.

Signs offered customers the opportunity to learn basic sign language by way of graphics on the menu, as well as cheat sheets placed strategically around the restaurant to make ordering easier for those who did not know sign language. With a majority deaf wait staff, it was expected that customers, all customers, would order in sign language. "We want to create awareness for the hearing community that the deaf community has the ability to do anything and everything," says manager Rachel Shemuel. "It's also a good opportunity for the hearing community to see exactly what it is the deaf community go through on a day-to-day basis."[5]

All in all, the restaurant was able to employ nearly forty deaf employees, an extraordinary amount of job creation, particularly for a deaf community, where quality jobs are impossibly hard to come by. Christine Nelson, from the Bob Rumball Centre for the Deaf, called the project "super inspiring," and added, "We're thrilled to see something like this take place."[6]

Anjan Manikumar is a disruptor. First, he was uncomfortable with the service deaf customers were getting in his restaurant, so he taught himself sign language in order for a new truth to be born. In doing so, he discovered another, larger truth that made him even more uncomfortable: life as a deaf person is very difficult, particularly when it comes to being appropriately employed. So he showed up, took action, and birthed a new truth: creating a new kind of restaurant that embraced the many gifts of the deaf rather than dismissing them (unintentionally or not) as incapable of performing quality work as capable employees.

Signs restaurant faced some significant challenges to becoming successful by the standard measuring sticks of the business world. This included an enormous cost to train their staff (almost none of them had ever worked in the service industry and many of them had never even been employed before!), among other challenges. Sadly, one of the other objections the restaurant faced was discrimination from customers who did not want to be bothered with the hassle of having to order their food and drinks in sign language. "Many walk-ins would turn around and walk out when they realized the staff was deaf,"[7] Manikumar said. I cannot imagine how that must have felt for those hard-working waiters and waitresses, or the owner who was fighting to keep his business alive.

Unfortunately, the many challenges faced by the Signs restaurant were ultimately too much to overcome. They closed their doors in December of 2016, just a little over two years after opening them so wide to both their customers and the deaf community. Anjan himself is the one who told me about the closing when we first corresponded by email. "Signs is no longer in operations. Would you still like to interview me?" he wrote. My response, as evidenced by the chapter you are reading right now, is that I absolutely still wanted to include his story in this book. Maybe now even more so! Because the value and success of disruption is never best measured by dollars made or bar graphs contained in annual reports. Rather, it comes from having the courage to act on a truth that makes you uncomfortable, regardless of the long-term outcome. This restaurant mattered then and it matters now because it responded to a legitimate and valid need. It birthed a new and better truth than had ever existed before. It created jobs, and a path to employment, where there was not one before. This very much matters. More than anything, the Signs restaurant is the kind of disruption that will spur other courageous and innovative people to dream bigger dreams of disruption in order to help even more under-represented groups of people, because disruption is not solely for successful ventures—it is for any venture that creates a new, needed world. There is no doubt the Signs restaurant did exactly that.

NOTES

[1] "Deaf to Work," accessed August 28, 2017, http://deaftowork.org/?page_id=6.

[2] Anucyia Victor, "World's First Restaurant Staffed Entirely by DEAF Waiters Opens with Sign Language Guides on the Walls to Help Guests Order Their Food," *Daily Mail*, November 11, 2014, http://www.dailymail.co.uk/femail/food/article-2829917/World-s-deaf-restaurant-Signs-Restaurant-opens-Toronto-Canada.html.

[3] Victor.

[4] Paulomi Patel, "Signs Restaurant Breaks Barriers and Creates Support with an All Deaf Staff," Anokhi Media, January 16, 2016, https://anokhimedia.com/signs-restaurant-breaks-barriers-and-creates-support-with-an-all-deaf-staff/.

[5] Sima Sahar Zerehi, "Restaurant Staffed with Deaf Servers 1st of Its Kind in Canada," CBC News, July 30, 2014, http://www.cbc.ca/news/canada/toronto/signs-restaurant-introduces-diners-to-sign-language-1.2722538.

[6] Lee Moran, "Canadian Restaurant with Deaf Servers Encourages Diners to Use Sign Language," *New York Daily News*, August 4, 2014, http://www.nydailynews.com/news/world/canadian-restaurant-deaf -servers-encourages-diners-sign-language-video-article-1.1890921/.

[7] May Warren, "Signs, Canada's First Restaurant Staffed Mostly by Deaf Servers, Closes for Good," *Toronto Metro*, December 21, 2016, http://www.metronews.ca/news/toronto/2016/12/21/signs-canadas -first-restaurant-staffed-by-deaf-closes-.html/.

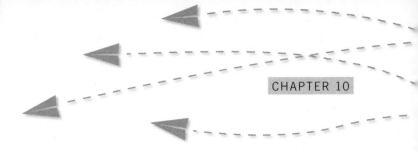

CHAPTER 10

Game Changer

If you are a "gamer," this will probably be your favorite story in the book. If you are not a gamer (I am not), I am asking you to hang in there with me on this one to the very end. There are some really fascinating things happening in the world of video gaming, and there is one woman right in the middle of it all.

Jane McGonigal is an author and video game designer who has made a name for herself over the last several years by positing that video games can have a spectacularly positive impact on just about anyone. But she is especially bullish on the positive impact video games can have on certain segments of the population who are suffering from some type of pain, trauma, or mental illness. She says it like this: Video games give a "real sense of optimism in our abilities and our opportunities to get better and succeed, and more physical and mental energy to engage with difficult problems. That is actually the physiological and psychological state of game play."[1] There are numerous statistics and studies she cites to validate this hypothesis, many of which she uses as illustrations in the popular TED Talk she gave in 2010 that now has nearly a million views.[2] Here are a few of the ones I found most fascinating:

- A game called *Re-Mission*, which helps young cancer patients stay motivated over the course of their long, difficult treatments. The game gives the young patients an opportunity to "fight" their cancer through video games the way the medicine is fighting in their bodies.[3]

- A game called *SuperBetter*, which is a "therapeutic and research tool" now played by more than five hundred thousand people. It allows someone to focus on something they want to be "super better" at in real life and pursue it in the game as a mechanism for being in control of their personal recovery/journey.[4]

- A game called *Snow World*, which has been used to help distract or refocus severe burn victims, reducing pain in some patients by 30–50 percent and proving to be a more effective pain blocker for some patients than even morphine.[5]

McGonigal's theory, and she has significant data to back this up, is that whether a video game is "good" or "bad" is all in the mind of the player. While video games are a form of escapism, which can be unhealthy, they can also be positive in the form she calls "self-expansion." While escapism could mean "running away from unpleasant thoughts, perceptions, and emotions, self-expansion is actively seeking new skills, stronger relationships and positive experiences."[6] To put it more plainly, the same video game might be used by one player to "get away," while another player might be using it to help themselves advance and learn positive skills that can help them outside the gaming console.

McGonigal became passionate about this type of game theory when she sustained a significant concussion in 2009 and began experiencing negative side effects. As a game maker and player, she began to treat her own recovery like a game, which she believes allowed her to heal faster and better. Thus the groundwork for her *SuperBetter* book and game were laid.

One of the most fascinating parts of her work is an area referred to as "gamification." This is where players will use techniques from gaming, including "multiple levels, points, badges and leader boards, to address realworld problems."[7] McGonigal herself has designed games like this—one where players had to survive an imaginary oil shortage and another where players worked with the World Bank to "support global efforts to ease poverty."[8] As a real-world application for this type of game, a group of alternate reality gamers actually used their gaming skills to try to find Al-Qaeda cells after the September 11th attacks.[9] In this way, you can see why McGonigal, and many others, are passionate about leveraging some of the best parts of video games into meaningful personal healing and growth in addition to world change.

Skeptics of McGonigal's work are far and wide. At best, they say she is mixing alternate reality and real life in ways that have been unnecessary for generations. At worst, they question her data and suggest it's nonsense. But McGonigal seems unswayed by the critics. "What I really want to do is help people suffer less. What games do successfully is help you tap into certain gamer traits . . . that are really useful to have when you're tackling a tough challenge."[10]

Let me confess: I am not a video gamer. I dabbled with video games some as a kid, and again with some roommates in college, but I do not think I have actually "beaten" a video game since jumping over the dragon and rescuing the princess all the way back in *Super Mario Bros*. Like, the original *Super Mario Bros.* on the original Nintendo. That being said, what McGonigal is attempting to do with video games, and honestly what she has done with some of her work already, is the very core of disruption. McGonigal was uncomfortable with the truth that video games could only be used for numbing pain. She believed there was a better way and experienced that herself after her own brain injury. From there, she began constructing new and better truths that might help gamers experience more of the positive sides of video games rather than only the negative ones. Some of the greatest challenges she faces without a doubt are the loads of negative press and research on how video games are creating damaging results in players rather than positive ones. But again, her willingness to dismantle those accepted norms and forge unimagined futures for video games is at the very heart of my definitions of disruption.

McGonigal's story reminds me in some ways of the story about the nursing home and childcare facility that joined forces. She is taking an institution of sorts (video games) and working to bring out its best qualities instead of its worst. I admire that about her work. Whether we like it or not, video games are not going away anytime soon. Each generation of children over the last two or three decades has played more video games and had more "screen time" than the one before them. I cannot imagine it is a bad thing to have very smart, passionate, and disruptive people working to leverage all of that game time into more healthy selves and a better world—which is precisely what McGonigal is spending her life working to do.

NOTES

[1] Tessa Berenson, "Why Playing Video Games Can Actually Be Good for Your Health," *Time*, September 26, 2015, http://time.com/4051113/why-playing-video-games-can-actually-be-good-for-your-health/.

[2] Jane McGonigal, "Gaming Can Make a Better World," March 17, 2010, https://www.youtube.com/watch?v=dE1DuBesGYM.

[3] Ken MacQueen, "The Interview: Jane McGonigal on How Video Games Can Heal," *Maclean's*, September 12, 2015, http://www.macleans.ca/society/health/the-interview-jane-mcgonigal-on-how-video-games-can-heal/.

[4] MacQueen.

[5] Philip Kollar, "Jane McGonigal on the Good and Bad of Video Game Escapism," Polygon, March 28, 2013, https://www.polygon.com/2013/3/28/4159254/jane-mcgonigal-video-game-escapism.

[6] Kollar.

[7] Bruce Feiler, "She's Playing Games with Your Lives," *The New York Times*, April 27, 2012, http://www.nytimes.com/2012/04/29/fashion/jane-mcgonigal-designer-of-superbetter-moves-games-deeper-into-daily-life.html.

[8] Feiler.

[9] Feiler.

[10] Feiler.

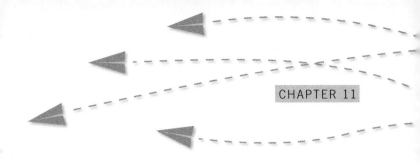

CHAPTER 11

Crazy College Kids

One of the most significant challenges facing undeveloped and developing countries around the world is access to acceptable medical care. This is especially true when it comes to mothers giving birth to babies. Even in the United States, with our plethora of resources, medical training, and access to equipment, labor and delivery can still be a very dangerous event for both the mother and the baby. It is fast-paced, ever shifting, and unpredictable—all recipes for disaster in countries that lack proper medical training and equipment. This is why the infant death rates in many less developed countries are many times over what they are in America. The good news is that there are many organizations and groups working to bring better training and technology to these places. The bad news is that it is not getting there fast enough, because we often try to bring our expensive and unwieldy equipment into environments for which it was not made and in which the people who are supposed to be using it have no idea how it actually works.

I have seen firsthand in our work in Ghana how quickly expensive equipment gets pushed to the side after it either becomes broken or is impractical in a setting where those expected to use it do not even fully understand what it is supposed to do. That's why I believe so deeply in the work and innovation of people like Jocelyn Brown and her team of bioengineering students from Rice University. This is their story of disruption.

One of the most important pieces of equipment in a labor and delivery room is called a CPAP (continuous positive airway pressure) machine. You have probably heard of this machine but not might be sure exactly what it does. Let me explain: the CPAP helps struggling premature infants breathe by forcing air in and out of their lungs.[1] In other words, this is a go-to piece of equipment in the neonatal unit of most every hospital in America. It is the hammer or screwdriver in their medical equipment toolbox. Unfortunately, the machines are incredibly expensive, at $6,000 each, which places them far out of the reach of most any developing countries' hospitals, particularly those in the rural areas. Enter Jocelyn and her team.

Jocelyn and her four teammates (Michael Pandya, Joseph Chang, Haruka Maruyama, and Katie Schnelle) were all a part of Rice University's hands-on engineering education program called "Beyond Traditional Borders." The problem they set out to solve (the truth they were uncomfortable with) was the reality that respiratory distress takes the lives of one million African newborns each year.[2] Many of those deaths could be prevented if the hospitals or clinics the babies were born into had a CPAP machine. But CPAP machines were too expensive to be distributed widely throughout these developing areas, so they had to figure out a new and better way to help these premature babies breathe.

Just nine months after beginning to work on the problem, Jocelyn and her team had their prototype. Two aquarium pumps in a clear plastic shoebox from Target later,[3] the students and their professors knew they might be on to something. Their suspicions were confirmed when they took the design on a trip to Rwanda, Africa. After demonstrating how the device worked, one of the Rwandan hospital administrators asked to buy the machine so they could begin using it immediately on their premature babies.[4] The total cost to build their design? Just $150 in off-the-shelf components—less than 3 percent of the cost of the ones used in most American hospitals.[5]

Over time, their device has undergone a number of changes and modifications to make it more practical and durable in the developing countries where it will be used. But the "Pumani" (meaning "breathe easy" in Malawi), as it has become known, is still made from primarily the same simple design Jocelyn and her team first came up with during that group project, and it is still incredibly affordable. Better yet, their innovative design has won several significant grants, which has allowed for product improvement and rollout across the country of Malawi, Africa. Clinical trials have shown the device can increase infant survival rate by 27 percent, which would have the potential to save nearly two hundred thousand African children annually if used across the entire continent.[6] Todd Mavende, from grant-awarding GlaxoSmithKline, had this to say: "This remarkable project shows what can be achieved through grassroots innovation, and we are delighted to be able to recognize the hard work of all involved. It is saving lives of Malawi's children today and can make a difference for millions of children around the world tomorrow."[7] A $150 machine, invented by college students for a group project using aquarium pumps and a shoebox, could save two hundred thousand lives a year. That is disruption at its best.

Perhaps the most meaningful effect of this new technology can be seen in the story of baby Chokonjetsa from Blantyre, Malawi. Weighing in at just over two pounds, tiny Chokonjetsa is alive today because of this simple breathing machine made out of cheap aquarium pumps. His name, which means "thrown away" in his native language, was selected by his grandmother because she did not believe he would be strong enough to survive.[8] Thankfully, she was wrong. Thankfully, Jocelyn and her team disrupted that truth before it became a reality for this family in Malawi. Thankfully, his family is just one of many whose lives will be saved, and therefore changed for the better, because of this disruption.

This story is one of the most powerful examples of disruption I have ever seen. It is altogether inspiring and humbling to consider what this group of young college students was able to do that is now having ripple effects across the entire world. It stands as a great reminder that big ideas do not have to be expensive or come from people who have already been in the industry for fifty years. Sometimes the best ideas come from people who are not afraid to try things that might not work. People unafraid of failing or looking silly. People who just cannot get comfortable with the idea of babies across the world dying because we cannot find a simple way to get a little air into their lungs. Disruption births new and better truths, and sometimes it literally helps keep new babies alive so that they have a chance for new and better lives.

NOTES

[1] Ayzh, "A Mighty Girl Congratulations Jocelyn Brown—Bravo to Innovative Women!" Facebook Post, April 4, 2014, https://www.facebook.com/AYZHinc/posts/617501528340382.

[2] Jade Boyd, "Clinical Study Finds 'Bubble CPAP' Boosts Neonatal Survival Rates," Rice Bioengineering, accessed August 28, 2017, http://bioengineering.rice.edu/Content.aspx?id=4294967819.

[3] Kelly Murray, "Aquarium Pumps Saving Babies' Lives," CNN, March 14, 2014, 2017, http://www.cnn.com/2014/03/14/health/aquarium-pump-breathing/.

[4] "Helping Newborns and Their Parents Breathe Easier," The Better World Project, accessed August 28, 2017, http://www.betterworldproject.org/search-stories/?pid=509/.

[5] Donald G. McNeil Jr., "Helping Newborns Breathe, No Spanking Required," *New York Times*, September 26, 2011, http://www.nytimes.com/2011/09/27/health/27breathe.html.

[6] "GSK and Save the Children to Help Roll Out Student-Created Breathing Technology in Africa," News Medical, November 15, 2013, https://www.news-medical.net/news/20131115/GSK-and-Save-the-Children-to-help-roll-out-student-created-breathing-technology-in-Africa.aspx/.

[7] Amy Kavalewitz, "Student-Created Breathing Technology Wins Another Award to Fund International Rollout in Three African Nations," Rice OEDK, November 14, 2013, http://oedk.rice.edu/news/1438309/.

[8] Murray, "Aquarium Pumps."

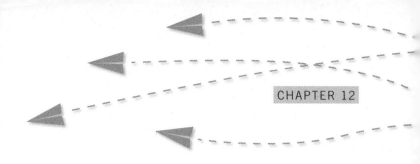

CHAPTER 12

Giving Away $7.5 Billion

Please do not stop me if you have heard this one before—because I am willing to bet the price of this book that you have not. This is the story I have most looked forward to telling since I ran across it doing research for this book.

It starts familiarly enough. Guy starts a business, business takes off, business grows, guy becomes a billionaire. But it takes a sudden and surprising (even shocking) turn when aforementioned guy decides to give all of that money away. Not after he dies; but while he is still alive. This is the story of Chuck Feeney, arguably the most generous person in the world and almost certainly the most generous person whose name you have never heard.

Chuck Feeney grew up in the small town of Elizabeth, New Jersey. He served in the US Air Force before attending college at Cornell University in upstate New York. After college he traveled to France, where he began tinkering in the business of selling duty-free alcohol to traveling sailors who were in the US Navy. The details of what happened next would fit better in a business book, so I will omit them here for brevity's sake. But that humble beginning of selling beer and liquor to sailors eventually became the DFS (Duty-Free Shop) you see prominently placed in most every airport in the world. The success of that business (an understatement) made Freeney billions of dollars. That's *billions* with a *B*. The success of that business landed him a number thirty-one spot on *Forbes*'s 1988 list of the wealthiest people in America.[1] What *Forbes* magazine didn't know, because virtually no one knew, was that Chuck Freeney was not actually all that wealthy after all. Yes, nearly all of his billions of dollars were gone. Legally removed from him. No longer at his disposal. Because he had quietly placed nearly every penny of his worth into a trust—not a family trust, a charitable trust. Even more audacious than that, his goal was to give away every dollar of that trust before he died. A dream called "giving while living." A dream he has spent the last thirty years executing to perfection. It is called the Atlantic Philanthropies, and its charitable work and generosity are unprecedented and its global impact immeasurable.

Chuck Feeney was uncomfortable with the idea that giving away just the interest on his mega-billions was sufficiently generous. He was uncomfortable with the perceived truth that only letting his money be used for good once he died was good enough. So he showed up, took action, and helped birth a new and better truth. It is a truth that is so large in scale it is nearly incomprehensible.

So how exactly does one go about giving away approximately $7.5 billion? It might seem like an easy task to give away that much money, but it is truly an enormous challenge. As a point of reference, just the interest on that much money would require giving away $1,000,000 per day, and that would not even shrink the original $7.5 billion. What Feeney has done is unprecedented not only for the amounts that he has given (which are staggering) but also for the precision and intentionality with which he has chosen to give. He has consistently leveraged his capacity and ability to engage others in order to multiply the impact of his donations many times over. Here is just a smattering of some of the ways Chuck Feeney's wealth has been shared with the world over the last thirty years:[2]

- $937 million given to his alma mater Cornell University, much of it to bring unprecedented innovation in science and research
- $370 million given to fund cancer research around the world
- $117 million given to support health care and civil rights in South Africa
- $350 million given to support a new New York City College of Technology campus on Roosevelt Island
- $20 million given to Operation Smile, helping children globally with cleft palate surgery
- Millions given for supporting peace building and reconciliation in Northern Ireland

- Hundreds of millions given to various other medical and biomedical initiatives

The list could go on, and on, and on—and it does. Through it all, Feeney has continued to seek ways to maximize the impact of his wealth and his life. Feeney, ever to the point, summarizes his giving like this: "I believe strongly in 'giving while living.' I see little reason to delay giving when so much good can be achieved through supporting worthwhile causes today. Besides, it's a lot more fun to give while you live than to give while you're dead."[3]

Amazingly, but probably unsurprisingly, Feeney's generosity has also served as inspiration for other billionaires and wealthy people in the world. Both Bill Gates and Warren Buffett credit Feeney for some of their most generous charitable foundation activities.[4] Gates says this about Feeney: "Chuck Feeney is a remarkable role model, and the ultimate example of giving while living."[5] Feeney is not quite as impressed with himself: "I simply decided I had enough money."[6]

One of the most common responses people have when they hear about the generosity of the ultrawealthy is to counter with the reminder that rich people can give all that away and still live much better lives than the average person. So consider this: Feeney, now nearly ninety years old, owns no house, owns no car, flew coach across the world until he turned seventy-five (and his family insisted for his health he move to first class), wears clothes off the rack, and wears a $10 Casio watch. He is, by every definition, a salt of the earth kind of guy. A man even more generous upon closer look than you might think at first glance. A rare and worthy find in today's world of facades and public veneers.

In December of 2016, with virtually no fanfare or media attention, Chuck Feeney's Atlantic Philanthropies wrote its last check. And while it did not bounce (as he famously joked to Warren Buffett that he hoped his last check would), it did mark the end of an era. An era of generosity, kindness, world changing, and financial disruption the likes of which the world has never seen.

Even if we do not have billions, or even millions, or even hundreds of thousands, Chuck Feeney's story should capture and challenge us to consider how we are using what we have today to make the world a better place. His commitment to doing right now what could have waited until later is inspiring. His willingness to go without things himself in order to help others around the world is astoundingly beautiful. His eagerness to do for others will leave a lasting impression far beyond his years here on earth. He said it best himself during the writing of that last check: "Our grants, now completed, are like sewn seeds which will bear the fruit of good works long after we turn out the lights at [our foundation headquarters]."[7] May the same be said for each one of us and our lives.

NOTES

[1] Steven Bertoni, "Chuck Feeney: The Billionaire Who Is Trying to Go Broke," *Forbes*, September 18, 2012, https://www.forbes.com/sites /stevenbertoni/2012/09/18/chuck-feeney-the-billionaire-who-is-trying -to-go-broke/.

[2] Bertoni.

[3] Robert Frank, "The Billionaire Who Stopped Giving," CNBC, July 10, 2012, http://www.cnbc.com/id/48139956.

[4] Bertoni, "Chuck Feeney."

[5] Bertoni.

[6] Steemtruth, "Billionaire Secretly Gives His Entire $8 Billion Fortune Away in 34 Years–True Story!" Steemit, accessed July 20, 2017, https://steemit.com/charity/@steemtruth/secret-billionaire-quietly -gives-his-entire-usd8-billion-fortune-away-in-34-years-true-story.

[7] Conor O'Clery, "The Irish-American Billionaire Who Gave Away His Fortune," *The Irish Times*, January 3, 2017, http://www.irishtimes .com/news/social-affairs/the-irish-american-billionaire-who-gave -away-his-fortune-1.2923497.

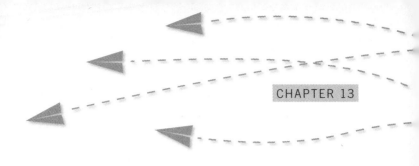

CHAPTER 13

Humans of New York

Brandon Stanton is the most famous artist whose name you have likely never heard. But if you have ever been on social media, chances are good you have seen his work—even if you did not realize it was his at the time. As the creator and founder of Humans of New York, his popular narrative-driven photographs have now been viewed by hundreds of millions of people around the world. He inspires and motivates millions on a daily basis. This is his story.

It all started when Stanton lost his job as a bond trader in Chicago. He says it was because he took too much risk and pushed too many boundaries.[1] Undeterred, he decided to take up photography and bought a nice camera. (His mother, for the record, was not happy with this turn of events.) "I just kind of made the decision that I was going to spend the next period of my life thinking not about money, but about how I spent my time," he said.[2]

But he did not head straight to New York City, as one might assume. Not yet. First he started with still portraits in downtown Chicago before moving on to take photos in other famous American cities. He shared these photos with a very small community of people on social media. But he learned quickly it was "his 'shots' of strangers and portrait work [that were] most appreciated online."[3] So he showed up in New York City with the audacious goal of "taking ten thousand street portraits to plot on an interactive map, creating a photographic census of the city."[4] This too morphed into something else, something better, and it was not long until Stanton was taking pictures of strangers on the streets and posting them online alongside a short quote from the subject. Over time, this grew into lengthy interviews with the subjects as Stanton dug down into what really made them tick. In capturing these real-life highs and lows from the human journey, Stanton also captured an audience of tens of millions of followers who were eager to "meet" his subjects and quick to identify with how much all of us actually have in common with each other.

One might wonder how easy it is to walk up to strangers on the streets of New York City (a city long known for its collective cold shoulder) to ask them for a picture and some meaningful information about their lives. The answer is *not very easy*. Initially, Stanton says he was turned down two out of every three times he asked someone for a photo. "The key is to be comfortable with the fact that some people are going to turn you down no matter what," he says. "That is why the work can be psychologically draining. But I'm used to it now."[5] Now, with more confidence and thousands of days of practice under his belt, Stanton's rate of rejection is down to just one out of every three. But it is the unlikely power behind the stories he does get that have made Stanton's work the stuff of Internet legend. So what exactly does Stanton do that is so compelling it has helped him publish two *New York Times* best sellers and earn a trip to visit President Obama in the White House?

Well, it is not that his pictures themselves are winning awards. Stanton is the first to admit his photos are anything but perfect.[6] But his fans are not tuning in for perfect photography. In fact, the imperfection of his shots adds to the charm of his entire project. What Stanton does best, what sets him apart and has helped create this loyal, global following, is talking to people in a way that gets them to share parts of their lives typically reserved for private counseling sessions (if at all). His gift is in getting random strangers to open up to him with their biggest dreams, most painful failures, and most vulnerable hopes for their lives. It is in this unprecedented vulnerability that Stanton has connected so genuinely with his online followers. It is, for lack of a less cliché explanation, the humanity of his Humans of New York photos and stories that has resonated so deeply with his audiences. While the stories might be different from their own, he is daily capturing these raw moments of real life. The fact that he puts them on social media, a place long accused of only getting the happiest parts of people's lives, is all the more counterintuitive. But it is working. People are connecting with the photos and one another in powerful ways not seen virtually anywhere else on the Internet. Stanton says it like this: "I think what Humans of New York does is highlights maybe the other tones of our lives that people aren't so willing to express, or tragedy that they might not have told anybody else."[7]

A few examples of recent Humans of New York posts to give you an idea what he means:

- A series of photos of a husband and wife married fifty-plus years when the wife begins suffering dementia and the husband stays by her side even when she no longer remembers him.
- An anonymous photo of an overweight woman's midsection and a quote about her boyfriend of twenty years not wanting to introduce her to his family or share intimacy.
- A Ghanaian immigrant who works at CVS talking about why he smiles all the time and loves his life in America so much.

As you can see, these are a broad range of topics and stories that touch nearly every emotion—and this was just three days' worth of photos!

So is Stanton surprised that people open up to him so freely about parts of their lives that surely must be painful and difficult to share? "I think that if you ask with a genuine interest and a genuine curiosity and a level of compassion, there's very little that someone won't share with you. I think the discomfort with sharing tends to be overridden by the appreciation of being able to distill the experience of your life into a story and share it with other people."[8] What Stanton has discovered, and leveraged so beautifully, is that our world is full of relationships that are a mile wide but only an inch deep. People want to be known, to be seen, to be heard, and to feel like they were listened to and understood. When we allow people that kind of space and freedom, there is no limit to how willing they might be to share about the deepest parts of their life with us—even if just for the touch of healing that comes with having one more person in the world who knows them more fully.

Stanton's disruption has come in many forms. He was uncomfortable with his own life being about money rather than purpose, and he was dissatisfied with spending his time and energy on things he did not enjoy. But his most powerful disruption was his willingness to slow down and really see people. He was uncomfortable with the truth that all these amazing people were passing him by every day, each one with great and valuable stories to share with the world, and he was missing them because he was not willing to have the courage to stop them and ask. So he showed up (with his camera), took action (photos), and now shares these new and beautiful truths with the world every day. In doing so, he is teaching all of us to slow down, really see one another, and remember that we're all a mix of a little pain, a little beauty, and lots of stories.

NOTES

[1] Anastasia Bow-Bertrand, "Brandon Stanton: The Man behind Humans of New York," Culture Trip, October 10, 2016, https://theculturetrip.com/north-america/usa/new-york/articles/brandon-stanton-the-man-behind-humans-of-new-york/.

[2] "In 10,000 Snaps of the Shutter, a 'Photographic Census' of a City," NPR, October 24, 2015, http://www.npr.org/2015/10/24/451184837/in-10-000-snaps-of-the-shutter-a-photographic-census-of-a-city.

[3] Bow-Bertrand, "Brandon Stanton."

[4] Bow-Bertrand.

[5] "In 10,000 Snaps of the Shutter."

[6] Barbara Benson, "Meet Brandon Stanton, the Man behind Humans of New York," Crain's New York Business, April 26, 2015, http://www.crainsnewyork.com/article/20150426/TECHNOLOGY/150429893/meet-brandon-stanton-the-man-behind-humans-of-new-york.

[7] "In 10,000 Snaps of the Shutter."

[8] "In 10,000 Snaps of the Shutter."

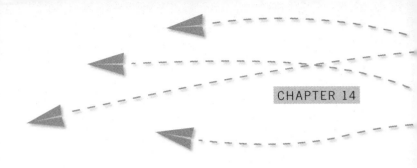

CHAPTER 14

Shelter Buddies

If you have ever been to a dog shelter, you know it can be one of the saddest and most pitiful places on earth. No matter how hard the shelter works to make the environment feel warm, safe, and inviting (and I believe the average shelter works tirelessly to create an environment that is precisely that), there are unattractive realities of housing hundreds of stray, lost, scared, and sick animals. These typically can be experienced in the piercing barks and foul smells that often permeate the area where the dogs are kept. Now there are many amazing stories that come out of animal shelters as well. One of those lives in our house, sleeps in our closet, has the worst-smelling gas I have ever smelled, and is named Wrigley. He is a yellow Lab we adopted at one year old from a local animal shelter, and he has been a part of our family now for more than ten years.

We cannot imagine a kinder or more gentle family pet, and all of our children (and Mom and Dad) absolutely adore him. But even ten years later we can still remember how it felt and sounded and smelled to walk through that animal shelter the day we got Wrigley. Walking past cage after cage in a never-intended animal prison can leave one feeling helpless or, at best, overwhelmed. Unfortunately, even if there were families lined up to adopt all the hundreds of thousands of stray dogs in our country (and there are not), many of the pups just are not quite ready to be with a family because of their anxiety, fear, and sometimes aggression. But one small animal shelter in Missouri is doing something disruptive to change that. They are forging unimagined new futures for these overlooked animals.

"A lot of times, dogs in a shelter environment are stressed by their surroundings," says Joellyn Klepacki of the Humane Society of Missouri. "It's unfamiliar and they don't know what's going on."[1] What this often leads to are dogs that stand in the back of their cage, far from where people pass by, and sometimes even with their backs turned. This is the dog's attempt to try to escape it all. "Unfortunately, these dogs are less likely to get adopted, since they tend to hang back instead of engage when potential adoptees come through."[2] It is a vicious cycle. Scared and anxious dogs stay at the back of their cages instead of coming to the front to meet people who might want to adopt them, and people are less likely to adopt them because they look scared and anxious and stay at the back of their cages. This means the most scared and anxious dogs often stay at the shelter the longest, which only adds to their stress and multiplies their ever-growing fear and anxiety. But what could possibly be done by animal shelters that are understaffed, short on funds, and always begging for volunteers to help fill the gaps just to maintain daily operations?

Enter the Shelter Buddies Reading Program. This innovative initiative brings in local school children, ages five to sixteen years old, and has them sit outside the front of the cages and read to the most anxious and scared dogs in the shelter. "While the kids read through their books, the shelter dogs, who are in desperate need of socialization, can acclimate to the presence of humans."[3] Klepacki explains it like this: "When a child comes in and sits down and they have calm energy and they aren't looking at the dog, it gives the dog the chance to check the person out and say, 'Hey, I feel comfortable. I want to go up and approach.'"[4] So that is what the children do. After a short training session to help them understand some of the signs and behaviors of an anxious dog, and after a short exercise to help them be more empathetic to some of the emotional challenges a dog in a shelter faces on a daily basis, the children sit down in front of the cage of one of the scared or anxious dogs and begin to read to the dog from a book. Calmly, kindly, and with the genuine innocence of a child, they read long books and short books and all kinds of books to these most vulnerable shelter animals. Along the way, the children become advocates and friends to the dogs. They watch them begin to feel more safe, they champion for someone to adopt them, and they celebrate whenever the big day does come for a dog to go to its new forever family.

One little girl who comes to read to the dogs at the shelter is named Alex. At eight years old, she is a budding reader using her own time to practice this important educational skill for the benefit of her furry friends. Alex is an aspiring veterinarian who begs her mom to drive the twenty miles to the shelter as often as possible.[5] Alex keeps a bag of books in her room so she can head to the shelter to read at a moment's notice. She even held her birthday party there, collecting toys and supplies for the animals rather than receiving toys and presents for herself. One of the dogs Alex read to was named Annie. Annie was a black pit bull mix described by the shelter staff as being "sullen and indifferent."[6] That did not last long once Alex got in front of her with that bag of books. "She was a shy dog, but she paid attention when I read to her," Alex said. "By the end of the week, she was so open and nice and polite." It was probably no coincidence that Annie was adopted and taken to her new home soon after Alex began reading to her. And Annie is not the only success story. Adoptions are now happening, on average, more than a week sooner for each dog in the shelter since the implementation of the Shelter Buddies Reading Program.[7] Now this might not seem like much to us, but if multiplied across thousands of dogs, in hundreds of shelters, this could open up tens of thousands of spots for more dogs. In doing so, it has the potential to save the lives of many, many future pets.

The best part may be that Joellyn Klepacki believes the program could "easily" be implemented in shelters across the country.[8] "We have a classroom for training, and we have a library of about a hundred donated books—that's it. For next to no cost, the payoff is immeasurable."[9] The part of the payoff that we can measure is dogs that feel more safe and are more likely to get adopted in less time plus children who are learning both connection with animals and the value of service to others. The fact that more shelters could easily replicate the program, and create this ultimate win-win for children and homeless dogs in their communities, is just the icing on top of the puppy treat.

The idea of bringing children in to read to scared and anxious pets at an animal shelter is disruptive in the best way possible. It takes an accepted norm and forges an unimagined future. It takes an uncomfortable truth (scared and anxious dogs are less likely to get adopted and therefore more likely to be euthanized) and ushers in a new and better truth. Dogs need to learn to be less scared and kids need to practice their reading. What is there not to love? Disruption, at its best, is taking old and tired establishments and "rules" and breaking them in ways that help people and make the world a better place. That is it. Sometimes it is complex and takes decades to bear fruit, and sometimes it is as simple as a child sitting down to read *Clifford the Big Red Dog* to a scared puppy in an animal shelter. Both are equally important, and neither require degrees or credentials to begin. The only prerequisites are creativity and the willingness to show up and start.

NOTES

[1] Katherine Hessel, "Humane Society Program Sees Kids Read Books to Shelter Dogs," *FOX2Now*, December 3, 2016, http://fox2now.com/2016/12/03/humane-society-program-sees-kids-read-books-to-shelter-dogs/.

[2] Embry Roberts, "Kids Get Shelter Dogs' Tails Wagging by Reading Them Tales," *Today*, February 25, 2016, http://www.today.com/pets/kids-get-shelter-dogs-tails-wagging-reading-them-tales-t76151/.

[3] "Kids Comfort Timid Rescue Dogs through Shelter Buddies Reading Program," Sniff & Barkens, March 04, 2016, https://sniffandbarkens.com/kids-comfort-timid-rescue-dogs-through-shelter-buddies-reading-program/.

[4] Hessel, "Humane Society."

[5] Roberts, "Kids Get Shelter Dogs' Tails Wagging."

[6] Roberts.

[7] Hessel, "Humane Society."

[8] Roberts, "Kids Get Shelter Dogs' Tails Wagging."

[9] Roberts.

CHAPTER 15

Easton the Great

Try to remember back to when you were fourteen years old (around eighth grade for most people). What kinds of things did you spend your time doing? Who were your closest friends? What were your hobbies? What did you enjoy the most? If you were like most teenagers (and like me), a large percentage of your time and energy at that age went into critically important tasks like talking on the phone with that cute classmate, spending hours in the bathroom perfecting your hair, defeating level 642 on your favorite video game, or walking the mall with your friends (but only actually spending money on fruit smoothies and Cinnabons). You might notice that schoolwork or other academic activity is conspicuously absent on that list. Now this is not to say that none of us ever worked on school-work or projects or applied ourselves to academics—that certainly happened at least here and there for many of us. But for most of us, and studies certainly back this up, our early teenage years find us being much more concerned with ourselves and our small circle of friends than we are about, oh, building something in our rooms that might disrupt a multimillion-dollar industry and help people around the world. That seems like a random example, right? It does . . . until you meet Easton LaChappelle.

Easton LaChappelle is from a small town in rural Colorado. How small? "This year's graduating class had twenty-three people," he says. "The nearest Radio Shack is an hour away."[1] So Easton found himself needing to find something to do, figuring out some way to fill his time. To say he used his time wisely is a bit of understatement. "With a pile of Legos, a spool of fishing line, some electrical wires and a smattering of plastic jointers and small motors,"[2] Easton created a robotic hand. The importance of his tinkering (Can we even call an outcome this amazing "tinkering"?) came when he met a young girl who was "transfixed" with his homemade prosthesis. He soon learned that she herself had been fitted for a prosthetic limb, but it was so costly that "it was almost a burden for the family."[3] At $80,000, it is safe to say it would be a significant burden for nearly every family and downright unaffordable for the majority of American families. Now while many might view the news of this enormous cost as a reason their homemade Lego contraption just would not cut it, Easton viewed things the opposite way. The feedback from the young woman compelled him to ask what was wrong with the current prosthetics industry that it would be so incredibly cost-prohibitive for someone in need to be able to afford what they needed. This is an amazing question for anyone to ask, but especially amazing when it comes from a thirteen-year-old boy in rural Colorado. It seems the answer to his question was that the bulk of the enormous cost came not from creating the physical prosthesis itself, but in linking the prosthetic device to the user's brain so that it could "capture what the brain was thinking and translate that into movement."[4] Now, again, most people would view this new bit of information as an enormous obstacle for moving forward—particularly someone with no budget, no financial backing, and a small bedroom in lieu of a scientific laboratory. Not Easton. He merely saw it as another problem he would need to solve to drive down the prices of prosthetics and help people like the young woman he had previously met.

His breakthrough came, fittingly enough, with the purchase of a video game from his local grocery store. The game "allow[ed] players to control a ball using the power of their mind."[5] Easton "took the game apart"[6] (I literally do not even know what that means) in order to see how different actions connected to specific parts of the brain. He then translated this new knowledge into the work he was doing on the new and improved prosthetic arm he was building.

LaChappelle, now twenty-one years old, has continued to push boundaries and challenge conventional thought in every way possible when it comes to his fight for a more affordable prosthetic option. "I wanted to make an arm that was lighter than a human's, but had the same strength—all the way up to the shoulder. I've achieved all that for a low price," Easton says. "The other half is the control system. It uses a wireless brain EEG headset that picks up 10 different channels of your brain."[7] Now when Easton says he achieved all of that for a low price, one is left to wonder if it is truly low or merely low compared with $80,000. The answer is truly low. Like silly low. Like unbelievable if not validated in multiple places low. LaChappelle's latest version of his prosthetic arm costs less than $400.[8] Adding to this powerful story of disruption is LaChappelle's commitment to getting this technology into the hands of anyone that needs it as cheaply and readily as possible. To that end, he made the technology for the arm openly available (open-source) on the Internet so that anyone who needs it can download the details and even make the arm themselves by way of using a 3D printer.[9] That is *Disruption* with a capital *D*.

So what is next for Easton? More disruption. He's already given a TEDx Talk to thousands, been to the White House to meet the president, and been invited by NASA to be an intern and help build a robot that will be part of a NASA space crew.[10]

Through it all, Easton's purpose and resolve has never wavered. "I just wanted to make something useful. This is what I was meant to do," he says.[11] Now that he has done that (a thousand times over), he wants to share his story with as many people—especially young people—as possible. "Inspiring younger people is my way of giving back."[12] With more than two million Americans living without a limb,[13] it is safe to say that Easton has already done something useful that will literally have a hand in changing many parts of the world that he will never fully be able to measure. In doing so, his story and resolve is inspiring people of all ages.

Easton's story might be the most obvious example of disruption in this entire book. He dismantled an accepted norm (prosthetics being exceedingly costly) and forged an unimagined future (prosthetics that cost 0.5 percent of the standard price and can be printed at home). Easton took a truth that made him uncomfortable (Why is this important technology so expensive?) and created a new and better truth. Because of that, he is changing the world in powerful ways. His disruption has a positive ripple effect that will bleed over into other industries, even beyond his own. His courage will inspire others to be more courageous in solving big problems to help people. I know it has inspired me, and I bet it has inspired you as well. That is the power of disruption.

NOTES

[1] Liz Presson, "Create Your Own Outcome: Easton LaChappelle Reinvents the Conventional Prosthesis," *Digi Blog*, July 1, 2013, https://www.digi.com/blog/community/create-your-own-outcome-easton-lachappelle-reinvent-the-conventional-prosthetic/.

[2] Josh Linkner, "How a 14-Year-Old Hacked the Human Arm," *Forbes*, June 18, 2015, https://www.forbes.com/sites/joshlinkner/2015/06/18/how-a-14-year-old-hacked-the-human-arm/#289b97781a4d.

[3] "The Teen Who Made a Revolutionary Robot Arm," BBC, October 26, 2015, http://www.bbc.com/future/story/20151026-a-teens-mind-controlled-arm-could-make-prosthetics-cheaper.

[4] "The Teen Who Made."

[5] "The Teen Who Made."

[6] "The Teen Who Made."

[7] Presson, "Create Your Own Outcome."

[8] Presson.

[9] "The Teen Who Made."

[10] Presson, "Create Your Own Outcome."

[11] Presson.

[12] Presson.

[13] Linkner, "How a 14-Year-Old Hacked the Human Arm."

CHAPTER 16

The Great Debate

Let's set the scene: there is a large stage in a big room. On one side of the stage sits a simple table with three chairs. In each chair sits a member of a college debate team. On the opposite side of the stage is a simple table with three chairs. In each chair sits a member of an opposing college debate team. In the middle of the stage sits a simple podium with a microphone. The audience is filled with a hundred people and a panel of professional debate judges. Sounds fairly straightforward, right? It mostly is—except this debate happens to be taking place in a maximum security prison in New York and one of the college teams is made up of three maximum security prisoners who are students at Bard College. The opposing team? Just three nobodies from some university called Harvard.

But before we go any further, you need to meet Max Kenner. He is the man behind this debate and the founder/executive director of the Bard Prison Initiative.

So what exactly is the Bard Prison Initiative? The Bard Prison Initiative is a "program that offers prison inmates a college-level liberal arts education."[1] Said another way, Max Kenner is the "prison reform activist who champions the transformative power of a college degree for inmates nationwide."[2] To put it into my own words, Max Kenner is the man who is attempting to disrupt the American prison system by empowering incarcerated individuals to dismantle the accepted norms of what it means to be a prisoner in America and forge an unimagined future for themselves, their families, and society at large.

Max Kenner was a sophomore at Bard College when he first dreamed up the idea of doing something to help people who had been incarcerated. "I just had this idea about tutoring and volunteering," he says.[3] "I picked up the phone book and just started calling people. I reached out to anyone I could," Kenner says.[4] From that simple desire grew something so much larger. Max had virtually no connections with anyone in the prison system or state and had never been to jail himself. What he did have was the enthusiastic backing from Bard College president Leon Botstein.[5] With Kenner's tenacity and commitment to seeing the project come to life, that's all he would need for the kindling sticks to create an unlikely inferno of higher education in the most unlikely of places.

In 2001, the Bard Prison Initiative matriculated its first class. The class had eighteen students, each one a maximum security inmate.[6] From that humble beginning, the initiative has only grown both in width and depth. As of late 2015, the Bard Prison Initiative had enrolled six hundred students, "virtually all serious felons with long sentences—many imprisoned at ages as young as sixteen, convicted of involvement in violent crimes."[7] Of those 600 students who have been enrolled, 350 have received Bard College degrees.[8] While the program is extremely competitive in terms of enrollment (only 10 percent of applicants are accepted each year, a figure comparable to the acceptance rate of Yale Law School), the students who are accepted have the opportunity to do something most of them never thought possible upon entering prison: learn skills and gain tools that will help them become productive members of society upon leaving the prison system. It's an investment that is paying off already. Less than 3 percent of those who earned their degrees from Bard are reimprisoned, which is remarkable by itself but even more so when compared with the 40 percent average from New York State.[9] Not only are these graduates not going back to prison; many of them are earning very respectable livings once they leave the prison system. A recent Bard Prison Initiative survey showed 83 percent of the program graduates as being employed (remember, these are convicted felons who have served time in maximum security prisons), with many earning between $40,000 and $80,000 in annual salaries.[10] These figures stand in remarkable contrast to a national prison system that has virtually complete bipartisan support as being awful at reforming inmates and even worse at preparing them for life after prison. The fact that the Bard Prison Initiative has done it with a group of people that many would consider the "worst of the worst" among those in prison just makes it all the more incredible.

One of the key pieces of information Kenner gleaned, even before officially launching the project back while he was still in college, is that funding for education in prison had been cut almost entirely back in 1994. "Prison wardens knew that ending college programs was terrible policy, but Congress did it," Kenner says.[11] Sadly, this means the single most significant obstacle in the growth of the Bard Prison Initiative is a lack of funds. While the program has in recent years begun to receive support from several prominent foundations,[12] a lack of support from both state and federal funding sources means their $2.5 million annual budget comes from the generosity of individual donors.[13] Perhaps in response to this economic reality, Kenner has encouraged "other colleges to establish their own programs. His vision had led to a sister organization, the Consortium for Liberal Arts in Prison, now exporting the concept to other states."[14] As of 2015, colleges in prison programs had been started in eleven different states across America.[15] It is incredible to consider what could happen if each one of the 2,474 public and private four-year universities in the United States decided they wanted to become a part of shaping the future of America in this important way. Compare that to the 5,104 local, state, and federal prisons scattered across America.[16] (The fact that America has more than twice as many prisons as four-year colleges feels incredibly depressing and should stand as the sole piece of evidence that we need to be more honest with ourselves about the fact that something—or a lot of things—we're doing in regard to our criminal justice/prison systems is just not working.)

Max Kenner and the Bard Prison Initiative epitomize disruption beautifully. He was uncomfortable with a truth (lack of prison reform and preparation for life after prison), so he showed up, took action, and stayed until a new and better truth had been born. Those new and better truths are in the form of hundreds of college graduates who now have an opportunity to do something amazing with their lives rather than continue the vicious cycle that too often seems to plague those who have been imprisoned.

Now that you better understand the Bard Prison Initiative, and the students who comprise the program, let's circle back to the scene we opened with at the start of this chapter—the big stage with a college debate team on either side. Bard College prisoners make up the team on the left and Harvard students make up the team on the right. This is, by the way, the same Harvard debate team that is the defending national champion for debate. Today's debate topic is "Providing Assistance to Undocumented Students," which the Bard College team must argue against. For the sake of brevity, I'll cut to the chase: the Bard debate team, made up of inmates from a maximum security prison in New York, defeated the illustrious and renowned reigning national champions from Harvard that day—a scene that must have made those in the audience feel like they were watching Rocky Balboa take down Ivan Drago in *Rocky IV*. This story is so amazing and surprising that it grew to be one of the most popular that year on the *Wall Street Journal*'s website.[17] It is a story that reminds us of the power of disruption. They might not all end this way, but it sure feels good when they do.

NOTES

[1] "Resolved: Debate Win for Inmates against Harvard Shows Benefits of Higher Education Behind Bars," *Democracy Now!*, October 30, 2015, https://www.democracynow.org/2015/10/30/prison_to _college_pipeline_program_at.

[2] Jerry Adler, "The Amazing Results When You Give a Prison Inmate a Liberal Arts Education," *Smithsonian*, November 1, 2014, http://www.smithsonianmag.com/innovation/amazing-results-when -you-give-prison-inmate-liberal-arts-education-180953041/.

[3] Howard Husock, "Should Prisoners Get College Degrees? This Program Says Yes," *Forbes*, August 13, 2015, https://www.forbes.com /sites/howardhusock/2015/08/13/should-prisoners-get-college -degrees-this-program-says-yes/#666cee416eba.

[4] Mallika Rao, "Bard Prison Initiative Founder Fights for a Cause," *The Poughkeepsie Journal,* September 8, 2016, http://www .poughkeepsiejournal.com/story/money/2016/09/08/young -professional-bard-prison-initiative/90092496/.

[5] Adler, "The Amazing Results."

[6] Adler.

[7] Husock, "Should Prisoners Get College Degrees?"

[8] Husock.

[9] Husock.

[10] Husock.

[11] Adler, "The Amazing Results."

[12] Adler.

[13] Rao, "Bard Prison Initiative Founder Fights for a Cause."

[14] Adler, "The Amazing Results."

[15] "Resolved: Debate Win for Inmates against Harvard."

[16] "Prison Policy Initiative," accessed July 20, 2017, https://www .prisonpolicy.org/.

[17] "Resolved: Debate Win for Inmates against Harvard."

CHAPTER 17

Disruption $1 at a Time

Mason Wartman left his job on Wall Street to start a pizza place in his hometown of Philly. But that's not enough to earn a place in a book like this. His pizza place (Rosa's Fresh Pizza, named after his mother) sells entire slices of pizza for just $1 each. Still not enough. His pizza place also uses a simple program based on customer generosity to feed a hundred homeless people a day in an environment where they can eat comfortably and free of shame. Now we're talking disruption!

Wartman was a twenty-five-year-old working on Wall Street when he sensed he had "plateaued as a stock researcher."[1] This left him with an important question: What should he do next? "To leave my comfortable existence, I had to outline basic goals for myself," he says. "I had always wanted to own my own business, and I thought I had developed the foundation for a successful concept."[2]

The business started like most businesses do: a big dream, lots of sweat, a significant amount of risk, and very little fanfare from anybody but your family. "The first couple of months . . . it was just me and some people showing up to make pizza by the slice for a dollar. We hit all the usual snags that new businesses hit. Personnel and product and trying to figure out how to make good food at good price and keep people happy."[3] It was about three or four months into the life of the new business when Rosa's Fresh Pizza diverted from the well-worn path of the typical start-up business.

A guy came in "having read about us in the local news, and he read that we serve a lot of homeless people because they can afford our food. He offered to prepurchase the next slice for somebody who didn't have the full dollar. There's a tradition in Italy where people can prepurchase empty cups of coffee, and the café will put an empty cup on a shelf behind the register, and anyone can poke their head in and redeem it with complete dignity."[4] In this simple exchange with an inquisitive customer, the future path of Rosa's Fresh Pizza (and thousands of homeless people) was changed forever.

Initially, customers would prepay for a slice of pizza and then place a sticky note on the restaurant wall to connote the availability of a slice to someone in need. When a homeless person would come in off the street, they could grab a sticky note from the wall and use that to "pay" for their meal after going through the line like everyone else. The concept caught on quickly, in spite of Rosa's employees never asking people at the register if they wanted to make a donation to pay forward a slice of pizza.[5] Before long, enough people were voluntarily making donations, and the word was getting out to enough of the homeless community that the small restaurant, with help from its generous customers, was feeding forty homeless people a day. But that changed quickly when Mason Wartman began to receive significant media attention and more people heard about his disruptive little pizza place in Philly.

"Three months after we started the pay-it-forward program, we were written up in the *Daily News*, which was a pretty big deal locally. They wrote a really good piece about us, and it got us a ton of attention," Wartman says.[6] But that was nothing compared with what happened next. Not long after that initial article, Rosa's Fresh Pizza and their disruptive program of feeding the homeless was featured on Upworthy with a video that received more than fifty million views.[7] Mason was also invited to be a guest on *The Ellen DeGeneres Show*. Once the dust had settled, in large part due to the increased media attention he received from Upworthy and the Ellen show (not to mention the help of a $10,000 check from Ellen), his little pizza place in Philly was able to begin providing meals to a hundred homeless people a day.

These days, the sticky notes on the wall in Rosa's Fresh Pizza are more "symbolic of everyone's kindness"[8] than they are functional. "We keep track in the register with a computer," Wartman says. "This way you don't have to write a single sticky note for each slice."[9] Also on the wall next to those symbolic remaining sticky notes is a smattering of brief open letters from the homeless who receive the gift of food to those who are giving it to them. It is a reminder of the rich connection that Rosa's is facilitating between those able to donate a slice of pizza and someone down on their luck just needing a break to fill their belly. One note says, "I've been homeless in Philly for six years, and I'm so happy to get to see people coming together and really making a difference in the community. Rosa's is a great start to changing the way homeless people are treated. God bless you all who contributed to helping us.—Swanko."[10] One paper plate attached to the wall says, "God bless you. Because of you I ate off this plate today. It is the only thing I ate all day. I am a homeless veteran and get treated rudely when I ask for help. Rosa's treats me with respect. Truly a blessing. Thank you.—Rob H."[11]

One important point Wartman wants to make about the success of this program in his little pizza place that gives back is that there is nothing inherently special about what he is doing that couldn't be copied by any number of other small businesses. "The business model of Rosa's is providing a basic necessity, something that everyone needs at a really good price, and letting other people buy it for people that otherwise can't even afford that. That's not applicable in every business but in a lot of businesses. A lot. It should be a practice that should be mimicked in a lot of other places."[12] He doesn't stop there, going on to say, "It is easily replicable."[13] It is worth pausing here to consider Wartman's call to action and reflecting on how many other businesses, even just those in the food and beverage industry, might be able to easily replicate something like this. While it would bring with it a certain set of logistical considerations, it would also present business owners and the patrons who frequent their businesses an incredible opportunity to give small bits of themselves and their wallets to help solve a significant problem that some number of real people in most every city face—not to mention the good that comes when the general public is given opportunities to interact more naturally with a group of people who are often hidden away (on purpose or not) in homeless shelters and soup kitchens. Normalizing homelessness, not as something to be aspired to staying in but as a reality of tough breaks, would be a significant step in our country beginning to address the issue and its many nuances more head-on. We can't be impacted by that which we cannot see. This might change that and, in return, change us.

Mason Wartman is a disruptor whose pay-it-forward pizza place is disrupting charitable giving, the relationship between the homeless and the general public, and the role of businesses in helping solve a community's problems. But there is one critical point here I do not want us to miss: Mason was not even the one who came up with this idea of disruption. It was brought to him by a customer. What Mason did, which is of crucial importance, was embrace this potential idea of disruption and see it through. Sometimes, maybe often, being a disruptor does not mean being the first one to come up with an idea. It does typically mean being willing to show up, take action, and stay until a new and better truth is born. Taking someone else's (really good) idea and embracing it yourself takes a special combination of humility and courage. Mason displayed a willingness for both, and

Philadelphia, along with many of the rest of us, is better for it. That's disruption.

NOTES

[1] Kathleen Elkins, "Here's Why One Entrepreneur Quit His Job on Wall Street to Sell Pizza," *Business Insider*, March 12, 2015, http://www.businessinsider.com/heres-why-this-entrepreneur-quit-his-job-on-wall-street-to-sell-pizza-2015-3.

[2] Elkins.

[3] Mark Shrayber, "Catching Up with the Man Who Ditched Wall Street to Serve Pizza to the Homeless," UPROXX, April 12, 2016, http://uproxx.com/life/mason-wartman-rosas-fresh-pizza-interview/.

[4] Shrayber.

[5] Shrayber.

[6] Shrayber.

[7] Maz Ali, "A Customer Walked into His Pizza Shop and Changed Philadelphia with One Dollar and a Post-it Note," Upworthy, March 3, 2015, http://www.upworthy.com/a-customer-walked-into-his-pizza-shop-and-changed-philadelphia-with-1-and-a-post-it-note.

[8] Shrayber, "Catching Up with the Man."

[9] Shrayber.

[10] Elkins, "Here's Why One Entrepreneur."

[11] Shrayber, "Catching Up with the Man."

[12] Shrayber.

[13] Elkins, "Here's Why One Entrepreneur."

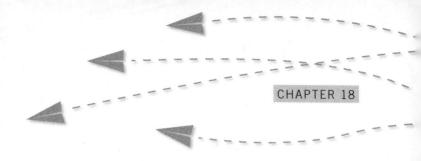

From Jail to Harvard

Disruption, as you have seen in many of the stories you have read already, often comes by way of a commitment to changing some external reality or truth that makes us uncomfortable. But this is not the only way it happens. There are many cases in which we may only be able to see the fruit of disruption that lives on the outside, while the original seeds that bore the fruit remain hidden on the inside. But there cannot be fruit without a careful and deliberate tending to the seeds that grow us into who we hope to become. This is especially true in the story of my friend Adam Saenz.

Adam was a little boy growing up with his family in the Rio Grande Valley of south Texas. When he was nine years old, his father left one day to "find work in Houston, Texas."[1] He never came home. Soon after, Adam began "running the streets" with his friends. If there was trouble to be found, they found it. Here is how Adam described himself:

> I was a sixth-grade Hispanic male from a single parent, low-income home. I had undiagnosed depression and was using street drugs to self-medicate. I had a history of interaction with the legal system, and spent most of my school days walking either to or from the principal's office for behavioral issues. Where there was a boundary to be pushed or a rule to be broken, I pushed and broke. As I became me, I drew an undeniable conclusion: I was grossly inadequate, somehow simply not capable of functioning properly in the world. My wisest option, I further concluded, would be to quit caring.[2]

After being arrested for drug possession as a sixth grader, something deep inside Adam told him he needed a fresh start if he was going to survive. He approached his mother and asked her if he could go live with family friends in Katy, Texas (just outside of Houston). So at the age of twelve, Adam left the Rio Grande Valley to move to Katy, Texas. On a map, it was a few hundred miles away. But in culture and lifestyle, it was a completely different world for young Adam.

"One of my main challenges was that I felt so different from everyone else," Saenz says. "I was living in Katy, Texas, a town with very few Hispanics, and I didn't even know them. So I felt isolated culturally. But I also felt isolated relationally. I wasn't living with my own family, and I was dealing with my own pain from everything I had experienced before I arrived in Katy. I had depression, self-rejection, and significant pain around my own trauma."[3] On the outside, Adam's life was better than it had been before. A more stable family meant more consistent food and other physical necessities. Even Adam's school experiences took an upward turn. He says his "grades were fine in spite of not having study skills or even knowing how to be a student."[4] But even with mostly As and Bs on his report card, Saenz said he "still didn't know how to gauge my academic progress because of all the background noise in my head and in my heart."[5] Saenz was still years away from learning to listen to and respond to that background noise that taunted him.

Adam graduated from high school with his peers, but rather than being excited about this accomplishment and all he had overcome to achieve this milestone, he was terrified about the future to come. "I knew I would hit rock bottom," he remembers. "I was leaving all of the structures that had kept my life in order. I was going to be on my own now, and I just knew I was screwed."[6] But it was in his early twenties that Saenz began to hear words in a religious setting that spoke of changed lives. It was there that he heard for the first time that he didn't need to settle for the life he had been living, that he could be something different. This message took root deep inside of him in ways that would shape and form him for many years still to come (and even still today).

This new message motivated Adam to start taking care of his business out in the real world. He got a job as a dishwasher at a local restaurant, moved into a garage apartment with a buddy, and bought a car to get to and from his work. (The car was a bargain at $400, and it was not until later he learned the car was so cheap because it had been used as a getaway car in a drug deal.) Life was looking up for Adam, and he felt so confident he marched down to the campus of the University of Texas at San Antonio and enrolled for his first college course: a remedial English class. Thus began an unlikely educational journey that would lead first to graduating from UTSA with a bachelor's degree in English (at the age of twenty-six because of his late start), then a master's degree in counseling from UTSA, then a PhD in psychology from Texas A&M University, followed by clinical training at Harvard and postdoctorate work at Brown.

So how exactly does one go from jail in the sixth grade to doctoral work at Harvard and Brown? What was the truth that made Adam so uncomfortable he showed up, took action, and stayed until a new and better truth was born? Well, it was not his drug use, his being jailed, nor his being separated from his biological family. It was not even his graduating from high school and being afraid of hitting rock bottom. Instead, in those formative years when he was in his early twenties, Adam became uncomfortable with his long-held beliefs about who he was and his perceived reality of the world around him. In his words, Adam realized that for virtually his entire life, he had believed "I am not good enough. I am not smart enough. The color of my skin is wrong. And I have no access to economic or social power or any opportunity to gain them in the future."[7] Adam Saenz had to learn to disrupt his core beliefs about himself and the world around him before he could even consider disrupting any of the outward elements of his life. "The things I believed about myself and the world were not true. But I held them to be true. In doing so, I allowed them to control me as if they were true,"[8] he says. Will you read that quote from Adam again for me? Slowly read it, maybe aloud. The things Adam held to be true (even though they were not) controlled him as if they were true. What a significant and meaningful discovery for a young man with Adam's background. As my professor Stephen Johnson once told us about the power of good preaching, "Words create worlds." In this case, Adam's perceived truths about himself and the world had created an alternate world—a world in which he was controlled by things outside of his control. With this as the basis and foundation for his belief system (not being enough and it not being his fault), there was no limit to the amount of self-pity, self-loathing, and self-rejection Adam could put on himself. If he was not good enough, and the world did not give young boys and men like him a chance, it is no wonder he would believe his behavior and choices did not matter because he thought he already knew the final outcomes! "Boys like me fail" is a painful and prophetic lie that can steal the future and hopefulness of even the most resilient. Thankfully, Adam's changing spiritual paradigm allowed him to see himself more honestly and truthfully as someone who could daily make choices to be in control of his own life and future. His disruption of these false truths in his life gave him a new path.

In addition to running a private counseling practice for a number of years, Adam began holding some behavior management workshops for teachers and educators. Over time, he grew tired of this topic and was ready to move on. For what he believed would be his last speech on the topic of behavior management, he chose to tell his own story of brokenness and pain and how, among other things, the power of a few teachers changed the road he chose to walk. The story was so impactful he was asked to come back the next year and give the conference keynote. From there, he wrote a book, *The Power of a Teacher*, which has now sold more than twenty thousand copies. He also found a new calling for encouraging and cheering on educators. His message to educators is simple and shaped by his key life experiences. "It's a message of 'thanks for believing in kids like me' and a message of 'you better take care of yourself too if you want to keep teaching,'" Saenz says.[9] It's a message that is clearly being well-received. To date Saenz has now given that message to more than three hundred different groups of educators around the country. Tens of thousands of teachers have now been impacted by the story of a hurting little boy from the Rio Grande Valley. This is the visible fruit of disruption born from the seeds of disruption Saenz has now tended to for many years. Over the next ten years, Saenz says he wants to become a more wholly integrated person "driven more by love than by fear." What a beautiful goal for each of us. It is a goal that requires disruption of the things we believe about ourselves and the world that are simply not true.

Adam's story inspires me, and should inspire you, because it is applicable to each and every one of us. All of us are held back by some false truths of our not being enough of something. To disrupt anything on the outside, we must first disrupt those uncomfortable (false) truths that quietly live within us—those mistruths that seek to devour and destroy our best selves from the inside out.

NOTES

[1] Adam Saenz, personal interview with the author, March 2017.

[2] Adam Saenz, "From Jail to Harvard: Why Teachers Change the World," *Huffington Post* (blog), October 6, 2012, http://www.huffingtonpost.com/adam-saenz/from-jail-to-harvard-why-_b_1747252.html/.

[3] Saenz, personal interview.

[4] Saenz, personal interview.

[5] Saenz, personal interview.

[6] Saenz, personal interview.

[7] Saenz, personal interview.

[8] Saenz, personal interview.

[9] Saenz, personal interview.

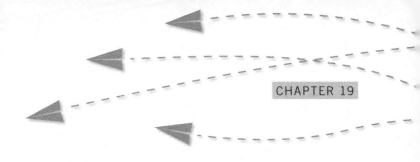

CHAPTER 19

It's Your Turn

We have spent the last eighteen chapters learning the stories of a number of different disruptors. These are all people who are alive today, are far from famous, and would not be recognizable even if they passed you on the street one night while you walked your dogs. They have ranged in age from five years old up to those nearing ninety. They have been males, females, white, black, brown, rich, poor, and everything else in between. The diversity of the stories, and that of the disruptors whose lives and actions wrote them, has been intentional. I wanted everyone who read this book, including you, to find a story (or five) they most identified with and that most inspired them. But inspiration only goes so far—it is a fleeting feeling based on emotion. Inspiration lasts a moment, a day, or maybe a week, but it is rarely enough on its own to incite deeply rooted and permanent change. The kind of permanent change needed to change the world.

It is too easy to get excited and inspired and sucked into the buzz of the big pep rally only to spill out into the busy hallways of life and immediately forget why exactly it was that we found ourselves feeling so excited in the first place. The pep band and cheerleaders and football team all disappear, and our inspiration seems to leave with them. I do not want this to happen to you. In fact, I will feel like I have failed you as your author and friend if that is all that happens to you. Disruption that changes the world will never come from merely reading the stories in this book. Not even if you highlight and underline and share your favorite quotes on social media and buy copies for everyone in your family (although that would be great, and I thank you if you do that). Disruption that changes the world will only come by understanding the common characteristics of these disruption stories and then applying those same values and priorities in your own life. Now this will look different for each reader, but the consistent values and priorities applied will be the same. They are the disruptive realities you must ultimately embrace if you are going to become a disruptor who changes the world.

The rest of this book is dedicated to helping you become a disruptor. This is where I walk you down from the comfort of your padded seat and ask you to stand next to me in the spotlight on the big stage. This is where the coach grabs you out of the first row of seats and tells you to take off your giant foam finger and grab a helmet because you are going in. This is where the broad journey to disruption funnels down into your personal journey to disruption. I am going to walk you, step by step, through my unique process of becoming a disruptor. This process is how I have managed to create so much positive disruption in my own life, and it is how the many other people featured in the stories of this book have done the same. What follows are the tangible steps that you can begin taking today to forge an unimagined future for yourself and the world around you. What you will read next is the very path that will help lead you from an uncomfortable truth to a new and better truth. This is your road map to disruption that changes the world. Lace up your boots— it is time to start.

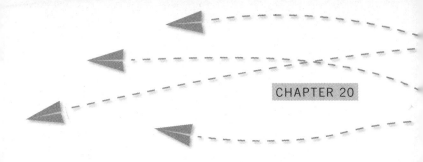

CHAPTER 20

Make a Commitment

In rural Ghana, far from the lights and noise of the more developed big cities, there is a powerful moment that often takes place when a visitor enters into a new community or village for the first time. Whoever greets you will first find an extra chair or bench (usually one of only a couple in the entire place) and invite you to sit down under the shade of the largest and most central mango tree in the village. Then word will spread from house to house that visitors have come. After a while (nothing is done quickly in Ghana, a characteristic I both love and hate about the country), the majority of the population of the village will be gathered there under that tree surrounding the visitor. The chief, or more typically his spokesman, will then ask a question in their native language that translates as this: "Tell us where you have been—and tell us where you are going." This question is a beautiful way of them asking, "Why are you here today and how do we fit into that story?" I think of this question often as I consider my own relationships with people here in America. I wonder how different my own family and friendships and acquaintances and business relationships might be if this was a question I was courageous and patient enough to ask more often.

This is the question I want to ask you today as we begin your own journey of disruption. Where have you been and where are you going? Or maybe more importantly, where do you *want* to go? Because the answer to that question will define much of what happens next. To understand the path forward to becoming a disruptor, you are going to need a MAP. This is your personal map to disruption, and it will be the basis of our entire journey and process to becoming a disruptor.

Here is your disruption MAP:

- Make a commitment
- Action plan
- Persist to transformation

That is it. Those three simple steps are all you need to understand and follow to forge unimagined futures, bear new and better truths, become a disruptor, and change the world. Let's unpack them one by one over the next several chapters so that you will be ready by the end of this book to begin writing your own personal story of disruption.

First, make a commitment. This is where we really begin to understand the first part of that question they ask in Ghana, "Where have you been?" It is in this self-reflection that we might begin to uncover some of the truths that make us uncomfortable. Making a commitment first means slowing down, being still, sitting quietly, and reflecting honestly on what truths in our lives make us feel most uncomfortable. Initially, this exercise is going to be very hard for many of us. We are really, really bad at being quiet and even worse at sitting still. But this is where the real work of disruption begins. If we cannot learn to sit still, then we cannot learn to listen quietly. If we cannot listen quietly, we will not allow our hearts to tell our brains the truth. If we cannot hear the truth, we cannot disrupt. So sit, be still, and be quiet. Find a quiet room, a closet, a back porch, a park bench, and be still. At first, just close your eyes, take deep breaths, and begin to calm yourself. Now I want you to clear your mind. As thoughts pop into your head, and they almost certainly will, imagine yourself physically picking up those thoughts and carrying them off to the side of your brain. You want to imagine an empty space with just a simple chalkboard or blank canvas in the middle of it. This is your map. The place where we will make a commitment to begin writing your new story of disruption. As you breathe, and as you intentionally work to clear your mind, you will find longer and longer spaces of time in which no thoughts come into your head. The brain is a most brilliant thing and will quickly adapt to what we are asking it to do. This is a good thing, because we have important work to do. After a few minutes of this, when you feel peaceful and calm, you can begin to ask yourself these types of questions: What truths makes me uncomfortable? What reality about my life or the lives of those around me or the lives of someone else in the world makes me uncomfortable? What bothers me about myself? What bugs me about my family relationships? What nags at me when it comes on the news or is talked about on the Internet? During these questions, keep a pad and paper nearby so that you can take notes. It might help initially to just start with yourself. What truths about myself make me uncomfortable? That question alone might stir years and years of disruption that make the world a better place because it puts you into a better place and helps bring forth a healthier version of yourself. Now there are no right answers here except the truth. This is not the time to hide from ourselves. This is not the place to eschew vulnerability. And if we just cannot help being dishonest with ourselves because the truths of our lives make us too uncomfortable? Then that is the first truth we must work to dismantle—we must be uncomfortable with the truth that we are uncomfortable dealing with the truth of our own lives. Your list of uncomfortable truths about yourself will vary as widely as the palette of colors we see in a field of wildflowers. But here are some of the most common ones we might find:

- I am uncomfortable with the truth of how I view myself.
- I am uncomfortable with the truth of how fear controls me.
- I am uncomfortable with the truth of my own arrogance/pride.
- I am uncomfortable with the truth of my selfishness.

- I am uncomfortable with the truth of my fear of deep connection.

And so on and so forth. We might walk out of this part of our reflection with just one or maybe fifteen different truths that make us uncomfortable. Don't be overwhelmed. This is a healthy exercise in understanding who we are and where we have been. We simply cannot begin to move forward to where we are going until we have done this part first, so that we might better (and more honestly) understand where we have been.

Once we have reflected on some of the truths about ourselves that make us uncomfortable, it is time to turn our attention to those outside of ourselves. Our families are a great place to move next. Here we want to ask ourselves questions like: What truth in my family makes me uncomfortable? What makes me uncomfortable in my relationship with my spouse or significant other? What makes me uncomfortable in my relationship with my children? What makes me uncomfortable in my connection with my parents or siblings or grandparents? Again, there are no right or wrong answers here. What we are seeking is the unvarnished truth that has not been whitewashed by our incredibly sophisticated ability to lie to ourselves. We often do this as a protective mechanism. But it is not healthy or sustainable. Some of the common answers we might find to questions about our families are as follows:

- I am uncomfortable with the truth of my lack of patience with my spouse.

- I am uncomfortable with the truth of the tone in which I speak to my children.
- I am uncomfortable with the truth of my lack of depth in connection to my kids.
- I am uncomfortable with the truth of my lack of honesty in my relationship with my parents.
- I am uncomfortable with the truth of how my busy brain keeps me from being fully present with my family.

And so on and so forth. Again, we might walk away from this part with one or a dozen different truths that make us uncomfortable. Don't be overwhelmed. We are going to prioritize later, and having more than we need on our initial list shows that we are being honest and vulnerable with ourselves. I would be more worried with a list of just two uncomfortable truths than I would be with a list of fifty!

If this is your first time to do this exercise, this might be a good place to stop for now. You are bound to have several truths on your list that make you uncomfortable, and we don't want to try to work on too many of those at a time. If this is not your first time to work through this process and you are returning to this section of the book after having worked through the suggestions provided, here are some more categories we can begin to work through:

- What truth about my work or career makes me uncomfortable?
- What truth about my friendships (or lack thereof) makes me uncomfortable?

- What truth about my personal finances makes me uncomfortable?
- What truth about the ways I do (or do not) steward and take care of my body make me uncomfortable?
- What truths about my willingness to take risks or have greater courage make me uncomfortable?
- What truths about my personal integrity or character make me uncomfortable?
- What truths about my eagerness to pursue my true passions make me uncomfortable?
- What reality of my world (locally or globally) makes me uncomfortable?

You see the point. There are literally thousands of questions we could ask ourselves, from our relationship with food, to the way we interact with our coworkers, to the time we waste on social media, as we begin considering how we will "make a commitment" to disrupting some uncomfortable truth in our lives. Asking these questions is a good and an important part of this exercise. But it's only the first step of several that fall under making a commitment.

Important note: The point of this exercise is *not* to induce guilt or legalism. Those things have no place here, and I reject them on your behalf. The point of this exercise is to create awareness that gives us space to usher in freedom and an abundance of life that does not currently exist. Again, finding truths that make us uncomfortable should not bring guilt or shame. Rather, the hard and messy work of this kind of reflection frees us from the lie of wanting to act as if we have it all together or do not need help from anyone. None of us have it all together; we all need help from others, and each one of us has truths in our life that make us uncomfortable. The sooner we name that truth, the sooner we can begin working on bringing a new and better truth to life.

Okay, let's move forward. The next step is to prioritize your list. Which of the truths on your list make you most uncomfortable? Said another way, which of the truths on your list can you not imagine living with any longer? In many cases, this will be a truth that has bothered you for some time now—a truth about yourself or the world that has slowly been bubbling up and is now ready to erupt since you have given it an honest look with fresh vision for change. This is the one with which we want to begin. (Having a hard time deciding? Relax. Pick one. Any of them. Let's start with that one and come back to the rest of your list later. You have your entire life to disrupt. . . . We just have to start walking down the road instead of paralysis by analysis.)

Now that we have prioritized the truths that make us uncomfortable and chosen the one or two we want to disrupt first, it is time to continue our process of making a commitment. The next part of our commitment is to commit to learning everything we can about this truth and how it came to be something in us with which we are no longer willing to live. Let's pick one from our list as a working example: I am uncomfortable with the truth of my lack of depth in connection to my kids. Once I have this example, I want to begin to unpack it by asking even more questions, such as

- Why am I lacking this depth of connection?
- Did I have lack of depth in my connection with my parents?
- Why do I feel like I am lacking this depth of connection with my kids?
- What might deeper connection with my kids look like?
- What resources or guides are there out there on this topic?
- Who do I know that models deep connection with their children?

These questions form the baseline of our understanding of this current truth that makes us uncomfortable. In other words, these types of questions (and their answers) are going to help us more fully understand the reasons we lack depth of connection with our kids. The answers to these questions will be critical to our action plan, so be sure to take the time to answer them truthfully and carefully and to take good notes. The final part of our making a commitment to disruption is to remind ourselves *why* this truth matters to us. For this working example, it might be a sentence like one of these:

- I want to experience the truth of deep connection with my kids because I did not have that with my own parents.

- I want to experience the truth of deep connection with my kids because I want to be close with them as they grow up and leave my home.
- I want to experience the truth of deep connection with my kids because it will allow me to know and speak truth over their true selves.

This sentence about *why* the truth matters to you is important because it's how we will begin our next step in our MAP to disruption.

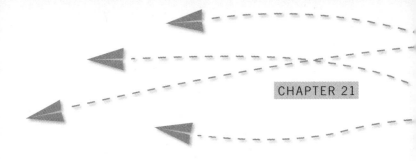

CHAPTER 21

Action Plan

Once we understand where we have been, it's time to begin working on where we want to go next. This is the action plan portion of our disruption MAP. If we think of this journey as going on a road trip, making a commitment involves understanding why we want a vacation and where we want to end up. The action plan is where we decide exactly what we have to do to get to our final destination.

To start, we want to write down our *why* reason from the end of the last chapter. This will guide us in our action plan, while also reminding us why we're working hard to disrupt. In other words, we want to keep reminding ourselves what is at stake here. Let's assume this is our *why* sentence about more depth of connection with our kids:

> I want to experience the truth of deep connec-
> tion with my kids because I want to be close
> with them as they grow up and leave my home.

That is what I write at the top of my action plan. Next, I take the things I learned during my information-gathering stage of making a commitment, and I have those resources and answers available to me during this part. Now I want to begin the task of turning those things into actionable steps that will get me from where I have been (shallow connection) to where I want to go (deep connection). If you are a visual person, you might actually find it helpful to draw it out like this:

[Start] Lack of deep connection with kids
[Finish] Deeper connection with my kids

What comes in between those two things (the start and the finish) is your action plan. Based on your answers to your questions noted previously, the research you did, and the role models you talked to who excel in this topic, these actionable items might look something like this:

1. Put my phone in my room when I get home from work every day.
2. Become deeply interested in at least one thing each of my children is interested in.
3. Set up individual dates with each of my children each month.
4. Have monthly meetings with someone I believe does this well. The purpose of our meeting is to share what is going well, to discuss what still feels hard, and to become encouraged by his or her experience/expertise.

These four steps make up the path between where I have been with my children (lacking deep connection) and where I want to go (deeper connection). Without these steps, I am just hoping where I have been magically turns into where I want to go. That is not a long-term solution and is highly unlikely to result in the disruption you are seeking.

Look at my list of actionable items and notice a few things: One, they are pretty specific steps. "Putting my phone in my room when I get home from work every day" is much more likely to be done than "Use my phone less when around the kids." Do you see the difference? Because it's a big one. Yes, putting your phone in your room (and therefore away from you) is a little bit harder from a control standpoint, but it is also much more likely to happen because it involves a specific decision or action that helps us get closer to our *why*. Next, numbers 1, 3, and 4 in the list provided include a specific time frame. This is important because it allows me to measure whether or not I am actually succeeding in my action plan to disruption. "More individual dates with my kids" is much harder to measure objectively than "Individual dates with each of my children each month." I either accomplished the latter of those two this month or I did not. There is no guessing or need to give myself half credit. Finally, the steps in the action plan provided are manageable. They are something I know I can commit to from a time, energy, and financial resource point of view. I did not list out thirteen actionable steps to deeper connection with my kids, because I know I will not remember or be able to execute thirteen things! But I know I can commit to doing four things. Especially four things that have a specific timeline and are measurable.

Healthy accountability on this action plan is an important part of this process. What is healthy accountability? Accountability that inspires and motivates and cheers on rather than induces guilt or shame (Are you picking up on how much I hate shame?). Healthy accountability is creating opportunities for people we love, and who love us back, to be able to check in with us regularly to see how we're progressing on our goals. The first step of this healthy accountability is being discerning about whom we actually trust enough to share these actionable steps of disruption. These should be the sorts of people who are already cheering us on and pulling for us to succeed in life. They should also be the kinds of people who do not need to constantly interject their own ideas and opinions about why something should or should not be important to us. While there is a place for that in life, I have found that it typically comes in less formal and more organic ways. Let me say this another way: We are not asking these people if what we want to disrupt should be disrupted. We are asking them to keep us accountable to the steps we've chosen to undertake to create a new and better truth. These check-ins can be weekly, biweekly, or monthly. They can be by text or phone or email or in person. The purpose is for you to share your hopes and dreams of disruption with someone who will cheer you on (and sometimes pick you up off the ground) along the way.

The final part of the action plan is probably the hardest. Once we've written out our actionable steps, we have to sit down with our road map and be honest with ourselves about what this path of disruption is going to cost us. Now in the example of my seeking more relational depth with my kids, the cost will almost entirely come in just time and intentionality. But there will be other things we choose to disrupt that will cost us much more. My wife and I had been working on opening a new school (nothing like it exists in our town or the surrounding towns), and it was costing us more than we thought it might—money, time, and energy. We often found ourselves pulling back, looking at one another, and asking, "Is this worth it?" For a long time, the answer was yes. The answer was yes because it's the type of education (nature-based, exploration-focused, no standardized tests, etc.) we want our kids to have for elementary school. However, the answer to that question become no when we found out my wife was pregnant with our fourth child. We've since handed this idea and vision off to someone else. Health boundaries and honesty with one's self are important parts of disruption.

Starting Mercy Project came at a big cost as well—mainly the risk of leaving my career and significant time away from my family as I have traveled back and forth to Africa more than thirty-five times over the last seven years. Is it worth it? Absolutely. But is it still a cost that we have to be honest about in our own home and with our kids? Absolutely.

In the same way, it is important that you count the cost of your actionable steps to reach the goals on your path to disruption. Being honest about what disruption is going to cost you will serve two main purposes: First, it will require some deep thinking and reflection on your part to make sure this is the right time and place and the specific truth you want to work on. This is important. Second, it will minimize the number of surprises you have along the way. If you know what is likely coming, and you have decided ahead of time it is worth it to you, then you are in a much better place when those inevitable challenges, obstacles, and objections do arise. If you haven't counted the cost beforehand, each one of those speed bumps feels much more difficult and painful than when you expected them all along. Ultimately, I have found that most people are still committed to moving forward on their path to disruption, even once they have counted and considered what it might cost them. But they are also much more prepared for reality, which makes them better road trippers along the way.

So we have remembered our *why*, created our actionable and measurable steps forward, invited people we trust to help keep us accountable, and calculated the cost of what the disruption is going to require of us. So what happens now?

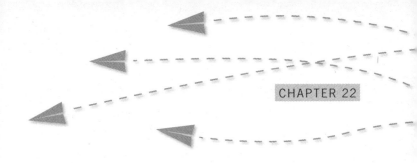

CHAPTER 22

Persist to Transformation

The last step in our disruption MAP is to persist to transformation. This is, as your grandpa probably said to you as a child, the part where "when the going gets tough, the tough get going." Here is the truth: disruption is not easy. Remember the definition of *disrupt* from all the way back in Chapter Two? *Disrupt* means to change the normal continuance of something. And I do believe ole Mr. Newton had some rule about it being harder to change the path of something than to allow it to keep going in normal continuance. (And if he didn't have that rule, well then he should have, with all due respect to a man who spent most of his life disrupting.) Disruption is hard, because if it were easy (say it with me), "Everybody would do it." So very cliché, yet so very true.

Persist to transformation means continuing along the path and journey to disruption even when it's difficult. This is honestly where successful disruptors separate from people who like the idea of disruption. Everybody is able to find truths that make them uncomfortable. (Listen closely—these typically come in the form of complaints.) Lots of people are good at sitting down and making goals, but very few people have the discipline and fortitude to stick with carrying those goals out all the way to the end. Disruptors know how to finish the task. They stick it out "until a new and better truth is born." It makes no sense to endure 8.5 months of a pregnancy (as the mother or father) only to leave before the baby is born. Yes, those last few weeks of pregnancy and then hours and hours of labor are hard. Yes, it is painful. But holding that new and better truth immediately makes all of that go away. Disruptors are committed to seeing things through, even when it costs something to get there.

But how exactly does one go about following through on a commitment they have made to forge an unimagined future or bear a new and better truth? What does persistence to transformation look like? This might not be the answer you are looking for, but it looks like rolling up your sleeves and getting after it. It looks like keeping your *why* in front of you constantly (on your mirror, posted on your computer, in your wallet, as a reminder on your phone, etc.). It looks like passionate pursuit of the *why* that you know is going to make a difference in your life and in the lives of those around you. If you forget why you want to disrupt, your will to be a disruptor will soon fade.

But you have to remember the stories of the disruptors who came before you and the fruit that was borne because of their willingness to persist. Think about the stories of just the disruptors in this book: inner-city kids who now have a future, cancer patients who can play a game to get well, homeless people with dignity to eat a meal, a grandmother who is alive and can chase her grandson, people who can print their own prosthetics for a couple of hundred dollars, and teachers who are inspired to take better care of themselves because a twenty-year-old disrupted his negative self-truths, and on and on.

None of these stories could have happened if someone had not chosen to persist. Persistence is the gasoline that makes the engine of disruption go! Let those stories inspire you and motivate you and push you forward to create the new and better truths that you want to see in your own life. Having the confidence and patience and willingness to persist is hardest to do before you have succeeded in your first disruption. After that, it becomes much easier because you have tasted the goodness and seen the shared beauty of that first new and better truth. After the first one, you can look back at your worn and tattered disruption MAP and remember not only the joys of the journey but also the joy of reaching that final destination.

People sometimes ask me if it is hard to persist in our work in Ghana, knowing there are still so many child slaves out there who still need our help. While we certainly would love to see more of the children become free, and while we work toward that goal every single day, we now have over one hundred children whose lives have been changed forever because we persisted. Children who are now going to school. Children who have been reunited with their families. Children who have new and better

157

stories of freedom because we persisted until a new and better truth could be born. Each one of these children will likely have children of their own one day. Most of them will probably have several kids. And the chances are very, very good that they will raise their children differently than they were raised because of the freedom they have experienced because of the work of Mercy Project. That means their children will likely not traffic their children, and so on and so forth until generations of Ghanaians have shared in the fruit that has come from seven years of persistence toward freedom. Do you know how long it was between the day I started Mercy Project and the day we walked out of our first village with any trafficked kids? 758 days. Our board and small staff persisted every single day for 758 days before we were able to witness our first new and better truth for child slavery in Ghana. But that persistence has paid off in the form of transformation in the lives of many poor fishing villages and many reunited families, because the passionate pursuit of persistence led the way.

I will spare you the time, but I could tell the same kind of story for the marathon I started here in my hometown. The persistence for creating that race (which most everyone said could not be done in a town so small) means that in just six years we have watched more than 40,000 participants cross our finish lines (many of them for the first time in their lives) and been able to give more than $700,000 to local children's charities from the proceeds of those events. Persistence! I remember one time when I was taking my then six-year-old daughter Micah on her weekly recycling route. It was cold, it was 8:00 A.M., and it was the day after Thanksgiving. There was basically no one on the streets of our neighborhood but us. She looked up at me and said, "Sometimes it feels hard to work. But it also feels good." That pretty well sums up what it feels like to persist.

Persistence to transformation is how the world is changed. This requires daily, sometimes hourly, commitment to the actionable goals you have set for yourself. This requires daily, sometimes hourly, reminders about the *why* behind your disruption. But over time, when you have a *why*, and you have actionable goals, and you persist, you will disrupt. It is a fact. While I cannot promise you exactly what the outcome of that disruption might be, I can promise you that you will become a different person along the way because you have committed to the journey of bettering yourself and the world around you.

On the disruption MAP, you will likely spend more of your time on the "persist to transformation" step than on either of the first two steps. Again, this is where we separate the people who like the idea of big dreams and bold visions from those who actually execute them. This is not a knock on anyone for not following through, but it is an honest reminder that this is where the hardest and most patience-requiring work happens on the path to disruption. Passionate pursuit of persistence to transformation must become a mantra and battle cry for those who are committed to disruption. But for those who are willing to persist, the new and better truths are waiting. They are truths that have the potential to transform you and the world for the better, and outlive your own lifetime. They are new and better truths that make the price of persistence along the way well worth it.

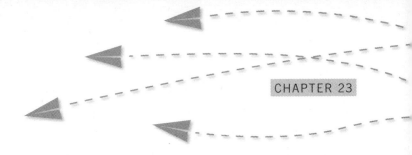

Overcoming Objections

Now that we've worked through the disruption MAP, I want to spend a few of our last pages together overcoming the most common objections most people have to becoming a disruptor, because I understand there are harsh realities that sometimes keep us from believing we can accomplish the tasks we desire to accomplish. So I will address the most common objections one by one because I do not want there to be any lack of understanding or excuses for anyone who reads this book. I want you to be able to set this book down and immediately begin your own disruption MAP. So please read on for what I hope will be some encouraging words as you begin your personal disruption journey.

Objection #1: "I don't have enough money."

Nope, we are not going to let you off that easily. While some disruptions do cost money, many (most!) of the disruption stories you read in this book cost little to nothing to begin. Correction: Most of the disruption stories you read in this book cost little to no money to begin. There is certainly a cost, but it is not in the currency you are thinking about right now. It is a form of currency that demands our time, energy, attention, and care. We all have this, more than enough of this, if we just choose to leverage it. But let's talk real dollars because I do not want anyone accusing me of sidestepping this objection: some disruptions cost money, but many do not. If you are passionate, committed, and willing to persist, you will find the money you need. Maybe it will be your own money that you have when you choose to go without something you used to believe vital. Maybe it will be money from a garage sale or a car wash. Maybe it will be money from something you sell that was collecting dust in the closet. That part does not matter as much as the effort to make it happen. If you want to pay for something you believe in, you will find the money. If you are not interested in finding the money, or having the sale, or going without, or working overtime, then whatever you thought about paying for probably does not matter that much to you. This is not me being rude—I am trying to be honest. It is too easy for us to claim something matters more to us than anything else but then be unwilling to sacrifice anything to see our dream come to life. That is just not realistic.

If your disruption requires investors or dollars from others, and some do, then you must show first that you are willing to personally sacrifice to make it happen. No one in the world will care about your disruption dream as much as you do—so don't expect anyone in the world to be willing to sacrifice as much for your disruption dream as you do.

One final thought on money: There is no lack of money in the world. There is a lack of passionate and courageous ideas that deserve to be funded. Solve the latter, and you will understand the truth of the former.

Objection #2: "I have little kids."

Hey, you and me both! During the writing of this book, my wife and I actually found out she was pregnant. So I took many evenings and weekends to write this book while helping parent a seven-, five-, and two-year-old, plus a sweet baby in the belly of a pregnant wife. It is not always easy, but it is possible. I am not superhuman, and there are millions out there just like me. Many of the disruptors in the stories in this book have kids themselves. That alone is not a good enough reason to not pursue a disruption dream you have growing inside of you. In fact, I think our children need and deserve to see their parents passionately pursuing things that matter to them. We have become a society that often caters so much to the needs of our children that we forget to live our own lives. Not only does this run the very real risk of birthing something unhealthy in our children, but it robs them of the joy of getting to watch their parents really pour themselves into something big and scary and audacious and important. Some of the best parenting work we can do is to allow our kids to see us dream big and then pursue those dreams—yes, even if it occasionally means we must tell them no. Now please do not misunderstand me. I am not suggesting that we become workaholics who ignore the emotional needs of our children. But I am suggesting there might be more for our kids to learn from being told no (with a purposed reason) than from always being told yes. Pursuing our disruption dreams, and letting our kids have a front-row seat while we do that, can teach them so many great lessons about passion, courage, confidence, doubt, fear, hope, and love, just to name a few. It is a privilege to model these things to our children, and I want to encourage you to share the journey openly with them. Sometimes this means sharing the wins with them, and sometimes this means sharing the losses with them. Kids need to see their parents fail so that they can begin to learn that (A) failure is okay, and (B) strong people get up again after they fall down. These are words we *tell* our children all the time, but pursuing a disruption dream allows us to *show* this to them in profound ways. Our kids will become who we show them they can become. Let them see you disrupt.

Objection #3: "My life is too busy."

I am not going to spend as much time on this one because I believe it is very similar to the answer to objection #1. We will always make time for the things we care the most about. In other words, the twenty-four hours in a day are enough for us to complete the tasks and projects that we hold closest to our heart. Now sometimes this happens incidentally: we look back at our planners or calendars and think, "Wow, I did not intend to spend so much time doing that." But those calendars and planners are mirrors.

They are objective, and outside truth tests us on what we value the most. If we believe in being healthy, we find the time to exercise. If we value our time with our spouse, we find a way to go on dates. Heck, I had some friends who could not get a babysitter one time, so they put their kids to bed and then sat with a baby monitor in their car in the driveway drinking wine just so they could reconnect with one another in a meaningful way. If something matters to us, really matters, we will find the time. Period. Hard stop. End of story. If work or school or something else is taking up so much of our time and energy that we literally have no minutes left in the day, then something is wrong. Our goal should be to put structures in place that allow us a healthy amount of work so that we have the extra time and energy to pour into the disruption dreams that matter the most to us.

Objection #4: "I didn't go to college / I'm not qualified."

Again, this is just not a universal truth that dictates success in a project. While I went to college, I had no experience with starting a nonprofit before I started Mercy Project. I literally Googled "How to start a nonprofit" and read articles telling me the kinds of things I should do. The same for starting the marathon. My one experience with being a race director was a local Turkey Trot 5K that had four hundred people and was so unsophisticated that my grandmother was sitting at the finish line scribbling down people's bib number and finish times. We did not even have names matched with genders, which is how I made the embarrassing mistake of awarding a fifty-year-old man named Jan second place overall in the *female* category.

Most of the people in this book did not have experience before their disruption. But that did not stop them. What they had was passion and chutzpah—two things college cannot teach you. Now do not get me wrong—I am not anticollege. I have two college degrees and am adjunct faculty at a major university. But I do not believe college is the end-all to be able to do great things. There are just too many stories that model a different path for me to believe that is the only way. College teaches you some very valuable lessons about responsibility and following instructions, but it does not define whether you have the courage and persistence and passion to disrupt a truth that makes you uncomfortable. You have much more say over that reality than any piece of paper on your wall. Experience is good, and practice can save you money and time. But nothing can substitute for good, old-fashioned "get out there and do it." So . . . get out there and do it!

Objection #5: "I'm too young / I'm too old."

Did you read the stories in this book?! Micah was five years old when she started her own recycling business. Mama Hill is well into her life and still disrupting by tutoring children in her little home in Los Angeles. Jocelyn and her team from Rice University were "college kids" when they developed a CPAP machine that might save thousands of lives in developing countries. The list could go on and on. When it comes to disruption, age is truly just a number. You are never too young, or too old, to become so uncomfortable with a truth that you choose to show up and stick around until a new and better truth has been born. The option to take that kind of action is available to each and every one of us, regardless of the year on our birth certificates.

I would actually argue that young people have an incredible opportunity to be powerfully disruptive because you have not become set in your ways yet. It really is true that "old habits die hard," which means that creating a pattern of disruptive habits early on is probably our best bet. Young people generally have less financial risk and more runway to catch up for time lost pursuing a career. I think right after college (if you go that route) is a great time to take a chance. Low dollars needed to live, no dependents, still full of energy and not jaded to the hard edges of the world—I love this stage of life to chase big dreams and do big things. And if you try and fail? You will never live with the wonder or "What if?" that so many others toss and turn in their beds about for too many nights of their lives.

Now for the older crowd—the group that has a few gray hairs, kids who can drive themselves around, and maybe even grandkids. First, thanks for reading this book. The fact that you picked this book up and have read this far says something about you and the kind of life you live. For you, age is also just a number. You are as young and full of life and energy and disruption dreams as you choose. There are examples all around us of people well into their later years of life who choose to live that last decade or two with more reckless abandon and courage than all the decades before combined. I love these kinds of stories. My own grandmother was nearly seventy years old when she came to help me at the camp I was directing for inner-city kids. Fanny pack stuffed like Mary Poppins's purse, she scurried around that camp during those hot Texas summers like a woman on a mission to love each and every person she came into contact with and to make their lives better. For four summers straight (ages sixty-eight to seventy-one), she did just that to the tune of sixty hours a week. Washing pee-drenched sheets, picking lice out of hair, and making more trips to Walmart than Sam Walton himself, she served tirelessly. To this day she says they were some of the best times of her life—times she would have missed if she allowed her age to define her activities instead of her heart.

Objection #6: "My parents won't let me _____."

Okay, this is a harder one. I am all about honoring our parents, and I believe you should be, too. The vast majority of us have parents who love us and care about us and only want to see us succeed. The rub comes when their definition of success collides with our definition of success. For many parents, success means a good job, a nice little sedan, and settling down to start a family. Now that's fine for many people. But it should not be pushed on to those who are not interested in that definition of success for their own lives. Sometimes, and you can especially see this in youth sports these days, parents are trying to live vicariously through their own children by pushing their child to accomplish the things they were never able to accomplish in their childhoods. This is not healthy, and most parents know this when they pause and really think about it.

But let us give your parents (and mine) the benefit of the doubt and say what they want from us is to be safe and have good lives. I appreciate this about my parents, and you should appreciate it about yours, too. But sometimes we have to help our parents understand that their definition of "safe" and "good lives" is different from our own. For many young people, being safe means taking measured risks but not choosing the path of no risk (which is an oxymoron, by the way, because any path naturally means we did not choose other paths, which is a risk of missing out in and of itself . . . but I digress). For many young people, a "good life" does not mean a cubicle, sedan, spouse, and 2.5 kids. It means a purposed or passion-driven life. It means a life of living for others and disrupting truths that make us uncomfortable, rather than sitting idly by in our own comfort and safety. This is a hard conversation, but it is one that is worth having with your parents. Letting your parents know the *why* in your disruption MAP may be exactly what they need to be able to further understand your motives and passion for taking the path less traveled.

Now there is some responsibility that falls on us here, too. It is our job to show our parents that we have a well-thought-out and measured plan that accounts for the reality that we might fail. I find it also helps if our parents see that we understand the risks involved and have hedged ourselves against those as much as possible. Finally, I think it can be extra beneficial to directly communicate that we are not expecting our parents to bail us out if we fail.

While you might assume this goes without saying, you might be surprised how many parents are driven by a fear that they will once again be responsible for you in some way that they are no longer capable of or interested in. But when they see you have a plan, that you can comfortably and calmly talk about the risks and possible barriers, and that you are not expecting them to bail you out, parents are wildly supportive and excited about the journey ahead. Sometimes they even admire your courage and risk-taking if it is something they were never willing to do.

"But, Chris, what happens if they tell me they will not let me do it?" Honestly, this is something you are going to have to navigate on your own. If you are under the age of eighteen, I suggest you honor your parents' wishes until you no longer live under their roof or require their financial support. But keep talking to them about it! Keep revisiting the topic and show them that it is not just a phase or a fad. Keep reminding them of your "why," and even invite them to solve some of the challenges and objections with you.

Objection #7: "My spouse won't let me _____."

I am going to hold all the jokes about who is the boss in the relationship and cut right to it: you need to prove to your spouse that this matters to you and that you are going to make sacrifices for it. It is not fair to ask your spouse to make as many or more sacrifices than you, so avoid that scenario if at all possible. Many of the strategies of communicating your disruption dream with your spouse are going to be the same as those used when communicating with parents, as described previously. But I have found that it really helps to understand why someone does not want us to do something, so that we can address those things specifically. A blanket "I don't want you to do that" is so much less helpful than a "I don't want you to do that because I am scared/worried/don't understand," and so on. When we have the reason, the facts behind their concern, we can be more empathetic and understanding. We can also speak more directly to their actual concerns. Both partners being onboard for a disruption dream is a critical piece of success. Rush this part or brush off your partner's concern at your own peril.

Objection #8: "I am scared I might fail."

First, thank you for being honest. Most of us have a lot more fear about all kinds of things than we care to let on. But being scared to fail when we are trying to change something very real and important about ourselves or the world? Of course we are! But let me repeat something I said very early in the book:

> I left my job and started as Mercy Project's lone employee on September 1, 2010. Truth be told, I was terrified. I had no idea what I was doing. I was overwhelmed by the scope of the problem. I was terrified with the thought of engaging an issue that seemed too large to actually solve. So what did I do with those fears and doubts and worries? I named them. Fear did not rule me because I gave it a name and called it out. I told

my wife, and my mom, and my best friends, "Man,
this is crazy. I hope this works." They affirmed and
encouraged and inspired me to pursue this vision.
They recalled my other crazy ideas that had
worked and reminded me that it would not define
me if I did fail. That failing, especially when pursuing something noble and good and right, was
okay—I would be the same guy after a failure that
I was before it. I needed to hear that. I used it to
catapult me forward as I leapt off that crowded
cliff of complacency to do a cannonball into the
sea of big dreams and bold ideas.

I feel fear, too. I am worried about failure, too. And sometimes I do and have failed. It happens. The key is to not let
those fears rule or define us. Name them, own them, and
work through them.

You are the same person if you fail as you are before.
Believe that. Here is the truth about failing: we typically
only care because we worry about how others might perceive us differently. Think about it like this: if you fall in
an empty hallway with no one around, you pick yourself
up and laugh about it. But if you fall in a crowded place
surrounded by people and care what they think about
you, your cheeks flush with shame and you burn with
embarrassment. The only difference in those scenarios is
the people who saw you fall (or fail). But that shows you
the power of how others' opinions and beliefs shape us.
We cannot let that happen with our disruption dreams.
It is okay to be afraid to fail. But that concern should be

couched in our concern over what failure might mean for our uncomfortable truth remaining true rather than in how others might perceive us if it does not work. That's the differentiator. As I said once already in this book, my life was changed forever when my desire to disrupt for good outgrew my fear of failure. You can choose the same.

Objection #9: "I like the idea, and I want to do it, but I don't usually follow through on things."

First of all, I sincerely appreciate your honesty. You are in very good company if you find following through on things to be a challenge. My gut, having spent time talking to hundreds of different people about the ideas in this book, is that the vast majority will like the idea of becoming a disruptor. Further, there will be many people who even have a truth or two that makes them uncomfortable. Some will even go to the trouble of drawing up an action plan. But the rubber will meet the road when it comes time to persist. This is, in my opinion, the great differentiator. Everyone has big dreams; few people are willing to persist and sacrifice to see those dreams come to life. Lots of people have bold ideas; not nearly as many are committed to the pain and struggle that comes with birthing these ideas into reality. Let me say it a different way: We see the stars on stage receiving their award, or the athletes on the field holding their trophy, and we think, "Wow, what a life. They have everything they could ever want." And while that may be true (I would argue many of those folks are just as discontent as many of us, but that's a topic for another book), it is unfair and naïve to look at their crowning career moment and not consider all of the pain it took to get there. A twenty-eight-year-old Super Bowl winner has been playing football for sixteen to twenty years of his life. He has played hundreds of games. He has lifted weights for thousands of hours. He has run bleachers and jumped on boxes and done burpees in the sand a thousand times. He has likely had multiple surgeries to repair parts of his body that have been broken or injured from slamming into other players over and over. He has watched films, eaten correctly, and maintained a healthy lifestyle for more than a decade. Most of us have trouble sticking to a diet and exercise routine for a month! I could go on and on, but I will spare you that. But I hope my point is made. A moment of disruption is often the crowning achievement of persistence that happens in the background—tireless, consistent, daily pursuit of persistence to transformation that might take place over years and years. This is why counting the cost after we make our action plan is so critical. "Is this something that matters enough to me that I will wake up every day willing to work for it?" If your *why* motivates you enough to answer that question in the affirmative, then let's go! If not, maybe find another disruption dream that fits that criteria. All of us will go in and out of seasons, and our passion and commitment to a goal may ebb and flow, but it has to really matter to us and be something we believe in if we're going to see it through. As the old saying goes, "How do you eat an elephant? One bite at a time." The same could be said of disruption. Daily, sometimes hourly, persistence to transformation—that's how you birth a disruption dream into reality.

CHAPTER 24

Go Change the World

Well, we made it. If you are reading this, that means you've either read through the entire book or you're one of those people who just flip to the last chapter to see how it ends. For my ego, let's just go ahead and assume the former of those two descriptions describes you.

You have heard some of my disruption story. You have read more than a dozen stories of ordinary disruptors, people just like you and me, who were willing to disrupt in a way that has changed (and continues to change) the world forever. You have even worked through some of your own ideas for the types of things in your own life that might need to be disrupted. So now comes the most important part of reading a book like this: the moment where you set the book down and get to work. This is where inspiration must turn into tangible activity. Where passion must spur us to action. Where excitement must begin paving the way for real outcomes. Because if this book is anything, it is a long way of asking you to become an agent of change in a world that desperately needs to be disrupted. It is a paper-and-ink request for you to dream big dreams of disruption and then actually go out and live them.

So go. Go change the world. Go disrupt uncomfortable truths. Go birth new and better truths. Go dismantle accepted norms. Go forge unimagined futures. Go write your own story of disruption. I may not know you, but I do believe in you, because I believe every single one of us has unique gifts and longings and passions and hopes that will lead to living out disruption dreams that will change the world and us. It just requires a little courage. So go and be courageous. The world is counting on you. Disrupt on, my friends.

> Visit the *Disrupting for Good* web page at
> www.meetchrisfield.com to continue the conversation
> and share your own stories of disruption.